Publication Manual

of the American Psychological Association

Special Edition

D1016104

PUBLISHED BY

THE AMERICAN PSYCHOLOGICAL ASSOCIATION, INC.

1333 16th Street N.W., Washington 6, D.C.

Publication Manual

of the American Psychological Association

Special Edition

Table of Contents

Publication Manual
of the American Psychological Association

Special Edition

Council of Editors[1]

American Psychological Association

The publication of scientific and professional journals is one of the major functions of the American Psychological Association. Its twelve journals embody the results of a vast amount of scientific, literary, and editorial effort, and also represent a substantial business venture. With the rapid growth of psychology, the number of manuscripts submitted to the journals increases year by year. There is, consequently, a growing need to conserve effort in the expanding enterprise of psychological writing and publishing.

The purpose of the publication manual is to improve the quality of psychological literature in the interest of the entire profession. The ultimate beneficiary is the reader of psychological journals whose time and energy are spared when articles are clear and concise. Most directly, the manual serves the authors of articles. Following its instructions will save many authors the trouble of revising and retyping manuscripts acceptable in content but not in form. The editors also hope to benefit

---

[1] Since its first appearance in 1952, the *Publication Manual* has proved its great value to the contributors to, and the editors of, the journals of the American Psychological Association. The exhaustion of the stock of the 1952 edition (1) late in 1956 made it necessary to reprint the *Manual*, with or without revision. The Council of Editors decided to prepare a new edition, in order to incorporate a number of revised editorial practices, recognize certain changes in APA policies, and clarify some sections in which the earlier edition did not succeed in making its instructions entirely clear to authors. An entirely new section on literary quality has been added (section 2) which should be useful to students and to a minority of contributors who need help with respect to certain essentials of composition.

Like the first edition, the 1957 revision is a joint product of the members of the Council of Editors. C. M. Louttit, late editor of *Psychological Abstracts*, was designated as coordinator, and completed much of the revision. After Dr. Louttit's death in 1956, the task was assumed by Laurance F. Shaffer, who had served as coordinating editor of the 1952 edition.—*Council of Editors:* E. G. Boring, L. Bouthilet, H. S. Conrad, J. G. Darley, W. Dennis, H. F. Harlow, A. W. Melton, *Chairman*, N. L. Munn, T. M. Newcomb, R. W. Russell, L. F. Shaffer, A. J. Sprow, and M. B. Smith.

by being relieved from the necessity of reading and returning many manuscripts which deviate from acceptable standards of style.

The collective authorship of the manual by the Council of Editors means that a greater uniformity of style will henceforth prevail in the Association's journals. It now seems desirable to eliminate all unnecessary idiosyncrasies due to historical accidents in the backgrounds of the journals. Authors who write for several journals will find the uniformity of style advantageous. The Council of Editors especially recommends that the manual be used widely as a guide for graduate students in the preparation of all papers.

The Journals of the American Psychological Association

The Association's twelve journals were acquired between 1925 and 1957 by gift, purchase, and direct initiation. As journals have been acquired and established, the Association has adapted its pattern of publications to fit the needs defined by the growth of psychology as a science and profession. The functions of some journals have been redefined progressively by formal actions of the Association or by informal processes of interaction among editors, authors, and readers. The present status of the evolutionary process is indicated in the brief descriptions of the fields of the journals which follow.

Authors are advised to study the fields of the journals before submitting articles to editors. It is important to examine carefully some current issues of the journals, and to read the information that most of them publish on the inside front cover. Much time is wasted when an article is sent to an inappropriate journal. Occasional articles may be appropriate to two or more of the journals, but in virtually all cases the author can select the journal most suitable for a given contribution.

The *American Psychologist* (monthly) is the Association's professional journal. A large part of its annual contents consists of the official papers of the APA: the program of the annual meeting, the reports and proceedings of the Council of Representatives, the reports of boards and committees, and news notes. It also publishes some articles submitted voluntarily. Appropriate topics for contributed articles include the following: the practice of psychology as a profession, methods and resources for graduate and professional education, the work, status, and earnings of psychologists, the relation of psychology to other professions, novel applications of psychology, and scientific articles of interest to psychologists in many fields. Preference is given to articles of broad interest which cut across the subdivisions of psychology. The section *Comment* publishes correspondence on controversies of current interest, as well as brief articles and notes.

Contemporary Psychology: A Journal of Reviews (monthly) began publication in 1956 as a journal of book reviews. It took over all book reviewing from the *Psychological*

Bulletin, the *Journal of Abnormal and Social Psychology*, the *Journal of Applied Psychology*, and the *Journal of Consulting Psychology*. The last named journal continues to review tests, but *Contemporary Psychology* covers books about tests. Short abstracts are avoided as belonging to *Psychological Abstracts*. Evaluative criticism is favored, and reviews are long enough to permit this sort of discussion. While all reviews are written on invitation, suggestions as to important books and appropriate reviewers are welcomed. The most important books, especially when they deal with controversial topics, may have more than one review printed simultaneously. There is a department, *Films*, in which educational and research films are described and assessed. A page of editorial comment discusses news about books and other matters that concern both book writing and this journal. Brief letters from readers and authors about the published reviews are welcomed insofar as space permits their publication.

Because *Contemporary Psychology* prints only reviews, many of the rules cited in this *Manual* do not apply. The editor supplies certain instructions with respect to literary style and form to each person who is invited to write a review.

The *Journal of Abnormal and Social Psychology* (bimonthly, two volumes annually) is devoted to both abnormal and social psychology. Its emphasis is scientific as distinguished from practical, and it is concerned with basic research and theory rather than with techniques and arts of practice. Abnormal psychology is broadly defined to include papers contributing to fundamental knowledge of the pathology, dynamics, and development of personality or individual behavior, including deterioration with age and disease. Articles concerned with psychodiagnostic techniques are evaluated with respect to their contribution to an understanding of the psychological principles of diagnosis; those concerned with psychotherapy are judged in terms of their contribution to an understanding of the therapeutic process. Case reports which serve to pose or to clarify important theoretical problems, or which promise to be useful in teaching, are often published. From the social area, this journal gives preference to papers contributing to basic knowledge of interpersonal relations, and of group influences on the pathology, dynamics, and development of individual behavior.

The *Journal of Applied Psychology* (bimonthly) favors manuscripts reporting original investigations in any field of applied psychology except clinical psychology and personal counseling. A descriptive or theoretical article is occasionally accepted if it deals in a distinctive manner with a problem of applied psychology. The policy is, however, to favor papers dealing with quantitative investigations of direct value to psychologists working in the following fields: vocational diagnosis and occupational guidance; educational diagnosis, prediction, and guidance at the secondary school level and higher; personnel selection, training, placement, transfer, and promotion in business, industry, and government service including the armed forces; supervisory training in business, industry, and government; biomechanics or design of machines to fit the human operator; illumination, ventilation, and fatigue in industry; job analysis, description, classification, and evaluation; measurement of morale of executives, supervisors, or employees; surveys of opinion on social or political issues; and psychological problems in market research and in advertising.

The *Journal of Comparative and Physiological Psychology* (bimonthly) contains original experimental contributions to physiological, comparative, and sensory psychology. Experiments utilizing human and subhuman subjects are given equal consideration. Physiological psychology is regarded as including correlational studies of any aspects of behavior and of the neurological and/or biochemical mechanisms underlying behavior. Theoretical interpretations of specific experimental discoveries are encouraged.

Council of Editors

The *Journal of Consulting Psychology* (bimonthly) is the clinical journal of the APA. It is devoted primarily to original research relevant to psychological diagnosis, psychotherapy and counseling, personality, and the dynamics of behavior. Although quantitative studies are given priority, relevant theoretical contributions, case studies, and descriptions of clinical techniques may also be acceptable. The journal publishes *Brief Reports*, which are one-page condensations of minor or specialized research studies, if the author will make a full report available in mimeographed form and deposit it with the ADI (see sec. 6.2). The section *Psychological Test Reviews* publishes descriptive and critical reviews of newly published tests, questionnaires, projective techniques, and other assessment methods of interest to clinical psychologists.

The *Journal of Educational Psychology* is devoted primarily to the scientific study of problems of learning, teaching, and measurement of the psychological development of the individual. It contains articles on the following subjects: the psychology of school subjects; experimental studies of learning; the development of interests, attitudes, and personality, particularly as related to school adjustment; emotion, motivation, and character; mental development; and methods, including tests, statistical techniques, and research techniques in cross-sectional and developmental studies.

The *Journal of Experimental Psychology* (monthly, two volumes annually) publishes articles intended to contribute toward the development of psychology as an experimental science. Experimental work with normal human subjects is favored over work with abnormal or animal subjects. Studies in applied experimental psychology or engineering psychology may be accepted if they have broad implications for experimental psychology or for behavior theory.

Psychological Abstracts (bimonthly) contains noncritical abstracts of the world's literature in psychology and related subjects. Unlike other APA journals, it contains no original articles and therefore solicits no contributions. Competent abstracters are almost always needed, however, especially to cover foreign-language journals, and books and periodicals in fields related to psychology. Abstracters are appointed by arrangement with the Executive Editor.

Psychological Bulletin (bimonthly) contains critical reviews of the literature in all fields of psychology, methodological articles, and discussions of controversial issues. Reports of original research or original theoretical articles are not accepted.

Psychological Monographs[2] (appearing at irregular intervals making an annual volume of about 500 pages) publishes reports of fundamental research. Preference is given to reports of comprehensive experimental investigations which do not lend themselves to adequate presentation in other journals. There is no fixed limit to the number of pages permitted in any monograph. An important programmatic study, for example, will usually require more pages than a less extensive research.

The *Psychological Review* (bimonthly) is devoted to articles in general and theoretical psychology. This area is obviously difficult to define, but preference is given to manuscripts which contribute broadly to fundamental concepts and theory. Papers that present surveys of literature, report experiments, or deal with applications are not ordinarily appropriate. The *Psychological Review* does not publish book reviews.

[2] A monograph in the *Psychological Monographs* series differs in some respects from a journal article. Its form is more like that of a book. Authors of monographs should consult the article by Conrad (8) and also note the special instructions given in sections 4.9 and 9.11 of this manual.

Publication Policies

Policies and practices have been established for the operation of the APA journals, either by formal actions of the governing bodies of the APA or through informal consensus and established custom. The procedures by which the Association controls its publication enterprises are stated in its By-laws, mainly in Article XVII, and also in parts of Articles III, VI, VII, XIV, XVI, and XIX. Interested readers and authors should consult the By-laws for information concerning the formal aspects of the management and operation of the journals.

Editorial responsibilities. The editor of each APA journal is responsible for its entire conduct, within broad policies decided by the governing bodies of the Association and rules of procedure adopted by the Council of Editors.

In addition to the office of Editor, the posts of Managing Editor, Executive Editor, Associate Editor, Consulting Editor, and Advisory Editor exist in one or more APA journals. These positions are defined as follows:

The position of *Managing Editor* of APA publications was established in 1950 at the Central Office in Washington. The managing editor and other staff members in the publications office of the APA are responsible for the technical editing and production of the journals.

The *Executive Editor* of *Psychological Abstracts* is responsible for the preparation of that journal, under policies determined with the aid of an advisory committee.

An *Associate Editor*, under the general guidance of an editor as to policies and procedures, is assigned a major and direct responsibility for the management of a defined segment of a journal. The segment may be a portion of a year, a topical area or department within the field of the journal, or a share of the manuscripts received. An associate editor, when requested by the editor, may correspond directly with authors concerning the acceptance, revision, or rejection of contributions.

A *Consulting Editor* or *Advisory Editor* (alternative, synonymous titles) advises the editor, upon request, on matters of the journal's policy, and on the acceptance, revision, or rejection of specific contributions referred to him for appraisal. He does not correspond directly with authors, but may draft statements for the editor to use in such correspondence.

Submission of manuscripts. Any qualified person may submit a manuscript to an APA journal. The author does not have to be a member of the American Psychological Association or to be sponsored by a member. Manuscripts are ordinarily submitted voluntarily on the author's initiative, although editors sometimes invite an author to submit an article. In no instance does an author receive remuneration. Manuscripts should be sent to the editor of the appropriate journal at his editorial office, not to the APA Central Office in Washington. The name and address of the current editor may be found in the most recent issue of the journal. Manuscripts must be submitted in duplicate.

Selection of manuscripts. A manuscript is judged by three main criteria: (*a*) it must make a significant contribution to an area of psychology appropriate to the journal to which it is submitted; (*b*) it must convey its message clearly and as briefly as its content permits; and (*c*) it must be in a form that will maintain the journal's integrity of style, and communicate to the printer exactly what he is to set in type. Manuscripts which do not fulfill the first criterion are rejected. Those which do not meet the second and third requirements fully are usually returned to the author for revision.

Articles in series. The APA editors discourage the publication of a series of articles based on a single research study for two reasons: (*a*) the reader's task is made more difficult than if a single, unitary article were published, and (*b*) space is wasted because of the duplication of introductory matter, description of procedure, etc. Serial publication may sometimes be justified, but only if each separate article deals with a study which stands logically and psychologically as an autonomous unit. Authors having articles prepared as a series should submit them at the same time to the same editor, who can then decide whether to accept them separately or to advise combination.

Duplicate publication. Articles which have already appeared in another printed periodical of general circulation are not acceptable. Legitimate exceptions to the practice of forbidding duplicate publication are recognized, however. Research done under contract with a government agency, for example, must often be reported in full in a special bulletin series published by the agency. Such material in abbreviated form may be submitted to a journal without prejudice.

The editing of manuscripts. Editors do not undertake the major editorial revision of manuscripts. Defective or excessively long papers are often returned to authors with detailed recommendations for their revision or condensation. Manuscripts which depart in appreciable degree from the style specified by this *Publication Manual* are invariably returned for correction and retyping. In all cases, the author is consulted about major changes. Minor changes, to improve details of expression or to correct minor errors of form, are sometimes made by the editor without consulting the author.

Order of publication. Articles are published in the order of their receipt, although they are sometimes accelerated or delayed by one issue. A common reason for the slight advancement or delay of an article is a need to fill an economical number of pages in a particular issue. Printers do presswork in "forms" of 32, 16, or 8 pages, and blank pages at the end of an issue are wasteful.

Certain exceptions to the rule of publication in order of receipt have been recognized by actions of the Council of Editors.

1. An editor may delay an article by more than one issue if the occasion for the delay involves some fault of the author.

2. An editor may advance or delay an article or articles by more than one issue for the purpose of assembling issues of homogeneous or highly related topics, if he indicates his purpose in an editorial note.

3. An editor may give advance publication, without cost to the author, to an article for any reason considered by him legitimate, provided this fact is explicitly recognized in an editor's note. Brief articles of comment and rejoinder are often given such advanced publication. More rarely, an article may be advanced because of its importance or timeliness.

4. The *American Psychologist* is exempt from the rule concerning order of publication because it must adapt its publication schedule to the requirements of official APA documents and reports, and may give prompt publication to articles whose value depends on their timeliness.

5. The *Journal of Consulting Psychology* gives early publication without charge to *Brief Reports*, which are one-page condensations of longer research reports of specialized interest or limited importance. Instructions for the preparation of Brief Reports, and a statement of the conditions governing their acceptance, are given on the back of the Contents page of each recent issue of that journal.

6. An author may secure the early publication of an article by paying the costs of publication, as described in a following section.

Date of receipt of manuscripts. Every published article is accompanied by a printed statement of the date of its receipt. This date is ordinarily the date of the first receipt of the manuscript, provided the author makes any required revisions in time to meet a deadline set by the editor. If the author fails to meet the deadline, the date on which the revised manuscript is received is considered the date of receipt, and publication order is determined accordingly.

Psychological Monographs, which deals with longer manuscripts, finds it impracticable to set deadlines for revisions. Therefore, the date of receipt of the final revision determines the order of publication.

The *American Psychologist* does not publish receipt dates. *Contemporary Psychology* does not publish the date of receipt of reviews.

Publication lag. The "lag" is the interval between the receipt of an acceptable article and its appearance in print. A lag of eight to nine months is considered optimal, because of the time needed to correspond with authors about revisions, to edit and prepare manuscripts, and to get them printed. It is the policy of the APA editors to keep publication lag within bounds by several methods:

a. By increasing the rate of rejection of manuscripts. This practice has the disadvantage, however, of setting relative instead of absolute standards, and of risking the loss of articles of value.

b. By insisting on the greatest brevity consistent with the adequate presentation of the material, and by returning excessively lengthy manuscripts for abbreviation (see sec. 1.2 of this manual).

c. By recommending the auxiliary publication of lengthy tables, figures, protocols, descriptions of procedure, etc. (see sec. 6).

d. By encouraging "early publication," which is described in a subsequent paragraph.

The cost of scientific publication. It is expensive to publish scientific journals. Their relatively small circulation and the complicated nature of the material they contain mean that there must be a continual struggle to produce and distribute them at prices their readers can afford to pay. The APA journals are self-supporting and their cost to subscribers is still moderate. The solvent financial structure of the journals is mainly due to the limitation of the annual pages of each journal to an economically practicable number.

Page allowances of journals. Each journal has an annual quota of pages, determined yearly by action of the Council of Representatives, on recommendation of the Publications Board through the Board of Directors. A journal's page allowance is primarily a matter of economics: balancing the costs of publication against the income from subscriptions. In setting a journal's page quota, consideration is also given to its publication lag, its rejection rate, the availability of other publication outlets, and the probable loss to psychology that might result from further delays or rejections. Each editor has an obligation to keep his journal within its page quota and to prevent publication lag from becoming unduly long.

Early publication. An author may secure more prompt publication if he agrees to pay the cost of printing his article as additional pages of a journal, beyond its normal quota of pages. An article accepted for early publication is inserted in the next issue to go to press, involving a lag of only from two to five months, with a median of about four months. To be accepted for early publication, an article must meet the editor's standard criteria of acceptability. The costs charged to the author are at a uniform rate per page for all APA journals, based on the average expense of printing. Information about the current charge may be obtained from an APA editor or from the APA Central Office.

By action of the Council of Representatives, the policy of accepting articles for paid early publication is followed by all APA journals except *Psychological Abstracts* and *Contemporary Psychology*, to which the policy is irrelevant, and the *American Psychologist*, which is given freedom to publish articles of urgent professional interest out of turn without charging the cost to the author.

Costs charged to authors. The author is charged the full cost of alterations or corrections, due to his own errors or preferences, which he makes on the proofs. At 1957 prices, the charge by printers for such corrections was at the rate of about $6.50 per hour. The author does not pay for the correction of errors made by the printer.

At present, authors do not pay any part of the regular printing costs of articles or monographs. In past years, authors were charged for a part of the extra cost of tabular material and figures in journal articles, and paid a fee per page for publication in *Psychological Monographs*. All of these charges to authors had been abolished by 1956.

Reprints. With the galley proofs, the author receives a reprint order blank, giving information about reprint prices. All reprints must be ordered when the proofs are returned, and the author is billed for their cost at a later date. Reprints are usually run off by the printer after the issue has been printed and mailed, and often do not reach the author until two or three months after the issue date. The APA journals (except *Psychological Monographs*) give 50 reprints of each regular article without charge to the author; however, the author is charged for any reprints of *Brief Reports* or for articles accepted for early publication. *Psychological Monographs* gives five copies of the monograph.

The Preparation of Manuscripts

The following sections of the manual describe the standards of style and form adopted by the APA journals. Some sections are concerned with the broader issues of organization, literary quality, and the preparation of informative tables and graphs. Other parts of the manual are devoted to more detailed matters of form, such as headings, abbreviations, footnotes, and the citation of references.

The requirements of style do not originate from the capricious whims of editors. The main reason why every manuscript must be invariably uniform in style is that printers are trained to "follow copy" slavishly. Printers set in type every letter, symbol, and punctuation mark exactly as it appears in the manuscript. Consequently, either the author or the editor must make the manuscript perfect before it goes to the printer—and editors prefer that authors assume the responsibility.

To permit indexing and reference, the following sections are numbered decimally.

1. *Organization and Writing*

1.1 *Organization*

The goal of scientific writing is effective communication. More specifically, its goal is to communicate abstract propositions, logical arguments, empirical observations, and experimental results, and their interrelationships and interactions. Clear organization is an especially important condition for such communication. Organization lightens the burden of the reader, and helps him to understand the author's intentions. In terms of Gestalt psychology, it helps the "figure" to stand out.

An article should be organized in terms of a formal outline which provides a clear and logical sequence of communication. The author's outline can be made apparent to readers by the discriminating use of headings (see sec. 3.3). The organization of an article that reports an experiment has now become fairly standard. The principal divisions of such an article are Problem, Method, Results, Discussion, and Summary. In some instances it is appropriate to use these words as centered headings, but more often the headings should be phrased to meet the particular requirements of a study.

1.11 *Problem.* An adequate exposition of the problem should state the questions asked and the reasons for asking them. In reports of theory-testing experiments, the exposition should state the theoretical propositions from which the hypotheses to be tested are derived, give the logic of their derivation, summarize the relevant arguments and data, and state formally the hypotheses to be tested.

1.12 *Method.* The method should be described in enough detail to permit the reader to repeat the experiment unless portions of it have been described in other reports which can be cited. This section should describe the design of the research, the logic of relating empirical data to the theoretical propositions, the subjects, the sampling and control devices, the techniques of measurement, and any apparatus used. Sometimes space limitations dictate that the method be described synoptically in a journal, and a more detailed description be given auxiliary publication (see sec. 6.).

1.13 *Results.* The section on results should give enough data to justify the conclusions. Special attention should be given to tests of statistical significance and to the logic of inference and generalization from empirical observations. Here again, auxiliary publication (sec. 6.) is desirable for supplementary tables of extended results.

    a. Authors are cautioned against inferring "trends" from data which fail by a small margin to meet the level of significance adopted. Such results are most economically interpreted as a function of chance, and should be reported as nonsignificant.

    b. When a study reports the concurrent or predictive validity of a method of measurement, the results must always show the degree of relationship between the measure and the criterion, and its practical value. The relationship should be reported in such terms as coefficients of correlation, cost-utility data, or expectancy tables. It is insufficient merely to show that the relationship is nonchance, in terms of the level of significance.

1.14 *Discussion.* The discussion should point out the limitations of the conclusions, note correspondences or differences between the findings and widely accepted points of view, and briefly give the implications for theory or practice.

Reports of research resulting in negative or unexpected findings should not end with long discussions of possible reasons for the outcome. Brief discussion is appropriate. Long "alibis," unsupported by evidence or sound theory, add nothing to the usefulness of the report.

1.15 *Summary.* Most articles, except very short papers, notes, and rejoinders, should end with a brief formal summary of the problem, the results, and the conclusions. If the summary does not exceed 130 words, it can often be used as the abstract of the article in *Psychological Abstracts*.

1.2 *Length of Articles*

The limited number of pages in APA journals available for an ever increasing number of manuscripts being submitted makes editors look with favor on brevity. Brevity, however, is not a good in itself, but when combined with adequate communication it is an ideal of scientific writing. Discursive manuscripts, which are longer than necessary to convey clearly to the reader the author's message, will commonly be returned for condensation. However, if lucid communication requires greater length, manuscripts somewhat longer than are ordinarily accepted will be considered on their merits, and will not be rejected merely because of their length.

1.21 *Standards of length.* The average length of an article varies somewhat from one journal to another, the range being from about 3,500 to 5,000 words, or about 10 to 15 pages of double-spaced typewriting. To maintain this average, critical scrutiny must be given to the length of every manuscript. Even an apparently short paper may be too long if its report can be made in fewer words. Long manuscripts may be acceptable if they have great merit, or if especially bulky materials such as verbatim transcripts of interviews are essential to their value.

Reviews of literature published in the *Psychological Bulletin* may be longer, but the upper limit is about 16,000 words unless special arrangements have been made with the editor.

1.22 *How to reduce excessive length.* Some practical suggestions for abbreviating articles are:

a. No attempt should be made to review the history or the literature of an area in the introduction or in subsequent sections of an article. The reader should be referred to previous summaries. Only the results and arguments required to provide the context for one's problem should be presented, and these in synoptic form.

Because many articles originate from masters' theses and doctors' dissertations, a word is in order concerning the difference between a thesis and a scientific article. A dissertation has the function of demonstrating the student's competence. Full documentation, historical development, complete tabular presentation, and reflective elaboration are often expected. A scientific article, in contrast, has the function only of communicating the author's original contribution. Lack of space and economy of readers' time compel the exclusion of other materials.

b. Every thought should be conveyed without waste of words or repetition. Discursive writing is the greatest enemy of brevity. Try rewriting each paragraph in reduced length, but with the same substance.

c. The economical use of tabular presentation is an efficient aid to brevity (see sec. 5.1).

d. Data should be presented no more than once. Although it is appropriate to refer to tabular data in the text of an article, care should be taken not to repeat data unnecessarily in the section on results, in the discussion, and in the summary.

2. *Quality and Style of Writing*[3]

Why should an article be well written? Is not the scientific task enough without adding a literary one? There are two answers. First, good writing is clear; it is precise, unambiguous, and economical. As a result, it tells exactly what you mean and reduces the chance that readers will misunderstand. Second, good writing is readable. It invites people to read what you have written, encourages them to continue, and makes their task easier. Writing may be a wasted effort if it is so formidable or repulsive that it frightens readers away.

To teach the art of writing is beyond the scope of the *Publication Manual.* It can only cite a few more comprehensive references, point out some faults often found in poorly written manuscripts, and suggest how to assess and improve one's style of writing.

2.1 *References on Literary Quality*

A brief but valuable reference on written communication is Daniel and Louttit (9, pp. 134–148). On the selection and spelling of words,

[3] This section incorporates portions of *Preparing Dissertations in Psychology: A Guide for Students,* prepared by the faculty members in psychology at Columbia University.

a good dictionary, such as *Webster's* (**25**), is essential. A dictionary of synonyms, often called a *Thesaurus* (**18**), is a good source of help in finding new words and in avoiding monotonous repetition, but it must be used with great caution to assure the selection of a word with just the desired shade of meaning. Fowler (**12**) discusses subtle distinctions of meaning, and delightfully explodes faulty and trite expressions. Some especially recommended articles in Fowler, which describe certain maladies of the inexpert writer, are: Elegant variation, False scent, Hackneyed phrases, Italics, Legerdemain with two senses, Love of the long word, Passive disturbances, Quotation, Repetition of words, and Unequal yokefellows. A good handbook of composition, such as the time-honored Woolley (**27**), offers aid on words, sentence structure, punctuation, paragraphs, and organization.

Readability is an old art which has only recently attracted the attention of science. Flesch (**11**), for example, has popularized a formula for reading ease based on the lengths of words and sentences. Flesch's approach has been justly criticized; he does not, for example, give any attention to sentence structure which is the most important feature of clear writing. Still, a consideration of his point of view will make you want to use short words instead of long ones when you can, and to keep your sentence lengths within proper bounds.

2.2 *Some Common Faults*

A few of the most glaring faults which editors often find in poorly prepared manuscripts are enumerated below.

2.21 *Long, awkward sentences.* Clumsy sentence structure is perhaps the most prevalent fault. A defective sentence can be improved and often shortened by removing nonfunctional words, by restoring a logical order, and sometimes by dividing it into two. Examples:

Bad: The development of psychodiagnosis is not best served as long as we do not follow further the question as to what it is that the psychologist should identify in order to diagnose pathology.

Better: The improvement of diagnosis demands a clearer definition of the behavior to be identified.

Bad: The lack of negative deviation in the pathological group, however, would not appear to be anomalous in view of scoring standards which permit the earning of mediocre scores by those who give responses involving a low level of abstraction.

Better: The absence of a negative deviation in the pathological group is not surprising. The lenient scoring standards of the test awarded moderately high scores to responses displaying a low level of abstraction.

2.22 *Short, choppy sentences.* A reduction of sentence length is not a universal remedy for incomprehensible writing. Sentences can be too short and too poorly integrated.

Bad: Normal people can respond both abstractly and concretely. Abnormal people can respond only concretely. This is shown by the Goldstein-Scheerer test.

Better: Normal people are capable of both abstract and concrete responses to the Goldstein-Scheerer test, but abnormal people are limited to one mode of response, the concrete.

2.23 *The indefinite "this."* A common fault is to begin a sentence with the word *this* whose antecedent is absent, vague, or distant. An illustration appears above in the bad example under *Short, choppy sentences.* An especially unfortunate practice is to begin a paragraph with *"This showed . . . . "* or *"This study showed . . . . "* when the antecedent may be any part of the preceding paragraph. The topic sentence of a paragraph should be comprehensible in itself, even at the cost of repeating a name or a concept, for example: *"Smith's study showed . . . ."* Within a paragraph, the use of the pronoun *"this"* should almost always be avoided. Adjectival use within a paragraph, as in *"This plan . . . ."* is sometimes unobjectionable, but *"The plan . . . . "* or *"His plan . . . ."* is usually better.

2.24 *Strings of modifiers.* An awkward and often ambiguous construction results when a long string of modifiers is placed before the noun modified. Replacing some of the adjectives with phrases is mandatory.

Bad: A new type motor skills performance college test . . . .
Better: A new performance test of motor skills used in colleges . . . .

2.25 *Faulty words.* The best word, of course, is one which conveys exactly the meaning desired. Technical terms must be chosen with care and used consistently. Nontechnical words offer a wider choice and a greater hazard. Scientific and scholarly writing is directed to a literate audience, and "difficult" words may be used when really needed to convey a precise meaning or to give variety. Always to be avoided are (*a*) pseudosophisticated long words which are no more precise than their short synonyms, (*b*) words warped from one part of speech to another and not yet acceptable to literary standards, and (*c*) colloquial expressions tolerated in informal speech but inappropriate in formal writing. A few illustrations are given; many other words are similarly misused:

Bad	Better
(*a*) Pseudosophisticated words	
is a desideratum	is desirable

| the methodology | the method |
| to utilize | to use |

(b) Warped parts of speech

to contact (verb)	to reach *or* meet
highs (noun)	high-scoring students
rigids (noun)	rigid subjects

(c) Colloquial expressions

a write-up	a report
a hook-up	a circuit
to separate out	to separate
a break-down of data	an analysis of data

2.3 *Some Requirements of Style*

The most basic requirement of style is adherence to the elementary rules of grammar and good usage. Psychologists who are already skillful and confident writers may follow their previously acquired standards with little hazard. For the less experienced, some explicit suggestions about the use of tense, person, voice, and number may have value.

2.31 *Tense.* Scientific reports are written mainly in the *past* tense. The literature cited has already been written, the study's procedure has been carried out, and the results have been obtained. Therefore, the references to previous research, the description of the procedure, and the statements of the results should be stated in the past tense. Here are some examples:

Literature: "Smith's study found (*not* finds) . . . . "
Procedure: "The judges were (*not* are) told . . . . "
Results: "The mean difference was (*not* is) 12.3 points . . . . "

Certain statements should be written in the *present* tense. A useful rule is that the present tense, in a research report, indicates statements which have continuing or general applicability. Definitions, statements from a well-defined theory, and hypotheses are stated in the present tense. In stating the results of an experiment, whether your own study or an earlier one, the past tense refers to *particular* results applicable only to a sample, and the present tense refers to *general* or timeless results applicable to a population as confirmed by tests of significance. Illustrative examples:

Definition: "Webster *defines* . . . ." "In this study, a discrepancy *is* defined as . . . ."
Theory: "The Gestalt theory *holds* that . . . ."
Hypothesis: "It *is* hypothesized that intelligence *is* (*not* will be) positively correlated with . . . ."
Result: "Jones *established* (past tense, particular study) that auditory stimuli *are* (present tense, general finding) more effective . . . ."

The future tense is rarely, if ever, used in a research report. Avoid the error of stating procedures and hypotheses in the future tense, as if writing a prospectus.

2.32 *Person and voice.* Scientific communications are generally written in the third person, a custom which often gives trouble to inexperienced and insecure investigators who think in the first person because they are so overwhelmingly concerned with what they themselves did, felt, found, or left undone. Such novices tend to an excessive use of *"we"* (a weak, inadmissible substitute for *"I"*) or else flee into an involved and clumsy use of the passive voice. The remedy comes from attitude more than from rules. A good and mature writer is so vividly aware of his material and of the ultimate reader that he perceives himself chiefly as a link between the two. To gain objectivity in writing, it is sometimes helpful to pretend that someone else performed the experiment, and that you are reporting what he did and found.

The passive voice is used extensively, especially in describing procedures. Do not, however, let the passive voice lead you into clumsy, involved expressions. Problems of person and voice are illustrated by these examples:

Bad: "We classified the subjects' responses . . . ." (*We* is faulty, unless it refers to two or more defined persons. Never use *we* as a substitute for *I*.)

Better: "The investigator classified the subjects' responses . . . ." (The statement tells who classified the responses, but without self-consciousness. Third-person references to *the experimenter* or *the investigator* are usual and acceptable. References to *the author* or *the writer* are generally avoided as self-conscious, except in theoretical argument. In book reviews, one refers to himself as *the reviewer*.)

Bad: "The classification of the subjects' responses was carried out by dividing them. . . . " (Clumsy use of passive voice. The writing is self-conscious, emphasizing the process of classifying.)

Better: "The subjects' responses were divided . . . ." (Better use of the passive voice. The focus is on the research, not on the researcher.)

2.33 *Number.* Verbs must, of course, agree with their subjects, and pronouns with the nouns to which they refer. Inexperienced writers often have trouble with plural words of Latin origin which end in -*a*, especially *data* and *criteria*. Although the word *data* may be evolving toward the status of a collective noun which may take a singular verb, conservative practice requires that it be treated as a plural word. The singular of data, *datum*, is rarely used. The singular of criteria is *criterion*, a respectable and useful word. Examples:

"The data *were* (*not* was) . . . . *They* (*not* it) showed that . . . ."
"Three criteria *were* used. *They were*. . . . "
"A criterion of senility *was* . . . ."

2.4 *Criticism and Assistance*

For many able research workers writing is a difficult and irksome task. It is better to seek both self-improvement and advice from others before submitting a manuscript than to hope that the editor will overlook faults or have time to correct them.

2.41 *Self-criticism.* A major cause of faulty writing is lack of self-criticism. Experienced writers correct their first drafts extensively; novices must learn to do likewise. Every paragraph and sentence should be examined with care, asking the questions: Is it grammatical? Is it clear? Is it coherent? Is it concise? Can it be made more readable? The entire draft should be read aloud to oneself or, better, to a person unacquainted with the content, in order to detect unclear expressions, clumsy sentences, and unpleasantly repetitive sounds. It is an imposition to send an article to an editor until the writer has made full use of his own resources.

2.42 *Securing help.* Almost all manuscripts should be given a "trial run" on a professional colleague, or better, on several of them. A review by others may evoke helpful comments about ambiguities or infelicities of phrasing, possible loopholes in the argument, or significant implications that have been overlooked. It is sound advice to authors never to argue with a colleague who finds a manuscript unclear. The reader is the consumer of a communication, and if one reader has difficulty in understanding the meaning, it is likely that others will also.

If an author has serious difficulties in expression, he may seek help from a competent critic who will help him improve his literary style. Psychologist colleagues who are skillful writers, and members of the English departments of colleges and universities, are often good sources of help. First, the plan and outline of the article need to be studied to see that they are clear and logical. Second, each paragraph and sentence need to be examined in detail and all faulty elements reconstructed. Help and advice on writing may save the author the disappointment of a rejected manuscript and spare the editors much trouble and embarrassment.

3. *Title and Headings*

3.1 *Title*

An article's title is important and should receive careful consideration. Its aptness is essential to later indexing and ready reference. Many papers are overlooked by subsequent workers in a particular area because of inaccurate or inadequate titles, and much research time is lost in checking articles with misleading titles.

3.11 *Titles should be short.* The title should convey the exact topic of the article, but need not specify all the variables involved. Do not try to cram a statement of the methods and results of a study into its title.

If an article becomes well known, the readers themselves will devise a short title. A psychologist will say to another, "Have you seen Smith's study of fear and learning?" He surely will not say, "Have you seen Smith's experimental study of the effect of fear induced by electric shock upon the instrumental conditioning of *Cricetus auratus?*"

The editor has to make a short title for almost every article to use as a "running head" at the top of right-hand pages. The author should help him by selecting a title short enough to serve that purpose.

Titles should never begin with phrases such as "A study of," or "An experimental investigation of." These words serve no useful purpose, and unnecessarily increase length.

While short, concise titles are generally preferred, it is recognized that in some instances as many as fifteen words may be needed to define the topic of the article.

3.12 *Typing the title.* The title should be typed, centered, at the top of the first page of the manuscript, with a margin of one and one-half inches above it. Type the title in capital and small letters, capitalizing the initial letters of all words except articles, coordinating conjunctions, and prepositions. Do *not* type it in all capital letters. It is much easier for an editor to indicate capitalization when he wants it than to indicate small letters when capitals have been typed. If the title is more than one line long, double space between its lines.

3.2 *Indication of Authorship*

3.21 *Author's name.* The name of the author, or names of authors, should be typewritten, centered, one double-spaced line below the title. Type the names in large and small letters, not in all capital letters.

Do *not* precede the author's name by the word *By.*

Omit all titles or degrees, either before or after the author's name. *Dr., Col., Ph.D., M.D., Assistant Professor of Psychology, Chief Clinical Psychologist*, etc. never appear in connection with an author's name in APA journals.

3.22 *Institutional connection.* One double-spaced line below the author's name, type his institutional connection, if any. The citation should be as brief as possible. In most instances only the name of the institution is required. Write *Harvard University*, not *Department of Psychology, Harvard University, Cambridge, Mass.*

When the author's main institutional connection is not with the Department of Psychology, it is often appropriate to cite his division or branch. Examples: *University Hospital, Student Counseling Center, School of Education.*

While brevity is important, cryptic abbreviations which may be unfamiliar to many readers should be avoided. For example, use *New York Regional Office, VA,* not *NYRO, VA.*

If an author has moved from one institution to another before a study carried out at the first location has been published, it is customary to list the new location under his name and to make acknowledgment to the former institution in a footnote.

In the publication of doctors' dissertations and masters' theses, it is customary for the author to list under his name the institution at which the graduate work was done, and to acknowledge his present location, if it is different, in a footnote.

A student or intern should secure the permission of his department head before listing his university or other institutional connection below his name.

3.23 *Authors without institutional connection.* An author who has no institutional connection lists the city and state of his address below his name.

3.24 *Multiple authorship.* If two or more authors of an article are located at the same institution, their names are typed on one line if space permits. Their institutional connection appears on the next double-spaced line. Commas separate the names of three or more authors.

If authors are from different institutions, the names should be on separate lines, the number of such lines being governed by the number of institutions. The name of the senior author (and other names from the same institution) should be the first line, then the name of the institution below; the second author (or authors) on a third line with the institution on the fourth line. Double space between all lines. The word *and* should precede the last author's name, on the same line.

Rodger F. Griessel, Donald C. Perkins

University of Alaska

and Nancy J. Sittig

The Nome Institute

3.3 *Headings*

The outline of an article, its major divisions and successively subordinate orders of subdivisions, should appear concretely in the manuscript as a series of well-chosen headings.

3.31 *Orders of subordination of headings.* The APA journals use as many as four orders of subordination in headings, but not all of them are required in every article. The four types of headings are, in order of precedence:

Order I. *Main* headings are centered, and are typed in capital and small letters, with major words beginning with capitals. They are not typed in all capitals. No period is used after the heading.

Order II. *Second-order* headings are also centered and typed with the initial letters of main words capitalized. They do not require a period. These headings should be used only in longer articles as described in sec. 3.32*d*; if used, write "Order II" in the margin.

Order III. *Side headings* are typed flush to the left margin, in capital and small letters without a concluding period. Text following a side heading starts on the next double-spaced line and receives paragraph indention.

Order IV. *Paragraph headings* are also known as "run-in sideheads." They are typed with a paragraph indention. They may have only the initial letter of the first word, or the initial letters of all main words capitalized; practice varies. They end with a period, and the text follows on the same line without extra spacing.

3.32 *Selection of headings.* Very brief and homogeneous articles may require no headings. If headings are used, the following rules should be observed.

a. *One* type of heading may be sufficient for a short article. In such cases, only main centered headings (Order I) should be used.

b. *Two* levels of headings meet the requirements of a great majority of articles. When two types are used, main centered headings (Order I) should always be selected, with either side headings (Order III) or paragraph headings (Order IV) as the subordinate level. Do not use Order II headings.

c. When *three* types of headings are required, they should be main centered headings (Order I), side headings (Order III), and paragraph headings (Order IV).

d. *Four* headings are suitable only for monographs, articles reporting a series of related experiments, and lengthy reviews of literature. They may use the four levels: I, II, III, and IV. The second-order centered headings (Order II) are avoided unless all four types are required.

3.33 *Avoid initial headings.* Initial headings such as *Introduction* or *Purpose* are superfluous, inasmuch as all papers necessarily begin with an introduction, however brief. Initial headings often spoil the regular appearance of the first page of an article.

3.34 *Numbering of headings.* The headings in articles submitted to journals should not be numbered or lettered. The varying styles of headings, and their arrangement, sufficiently reveal the organization of the paper.

The decimal numbering of sections of this manual is exceptional, intended to permit indexing and cross reference.

3.4 *Other Methods of Subordination*

In addition to the use of headings, two other methods are commonly used to reveal an article's plan and outline.

3.41 *Smaller type.* Details of apparatus and procedure, instructions to subjects and judges, case materials, and other subordinate matter, as well as all longer quotations (see sec. 4.74), are often set in reduced-size type. This practice saves space and distinguishes the material so set.

Material to be set in smaller type must be typewritten with double (not single) spacing. Do not give an extra indention to any of the lines of such material when typing it. Ordinarily, the smaller type is set the full width of the column or page in the journal.

Most editors prefer to make the final decisions with respect to the use of smaller type. Therefore, authors need only make sure that matter which might be set in reduced type is typewritten in appropriate paragraphs. The editor will add the instructions to the printer.

3.42 *Seriation of paragraphs.* Brief paragraphs describing successive steps of method, identifying groups, itemizing conclusions, and so on are frequently made clearer by indication of serial order. Number such paragraphs with arabic numerals, each followed by a period, but not enclosed in or followed by parenthesis marks.

3.43 *Seriation within paragraphs.* Seriation within a paragraph or sentence should be shown by small letters, in parentheses. Do not use numerals in parentheses for this purpose, because numerals in parentheses designate bibliographic references.

4. *General Style*

When an editor or a printer refers to "style" in a manuscript, he does not ordinarily mean its literary quality, but its observance of recognized canons of spelling, capitalization, punctuation, abbreviation, and the like. The most important requirement concerning style is consistency. The author of a book may have considerable freedom to choose his style, provided he is always consistent. Journals, in contrast to books, print the works of many authors on adjacent pages and must therefore have more definite rules if glaring inconsistencies are to be avoided. To give an extreme example, what impression would be created if the Vocabulary of the Wechsler Adult Intelligence Scale were designated within one issue of a journal as a subtest, a sub-test, a Subtest, a Sub-test, and a sub-Test?

Authors should take "style" seriously if their articles are to communicate effectively and to be acceptable for publication. There are several good references on style with which authors should be familiar. The University of Chicago Press's *Manual of Style* (23) is used widely. *Words into Type* (20) contains sections on grammar and word usage, topics not included in most manuals. Other useful references are the style books of the Government Printing Office (22), of the Modern Language Association of America (19), and of John Wiley and Sons (5). It must be noted that style books are often in conflict on minor issues. When there is disagreement, the instructions given in this manual hold for the APA journals.

The official dictionary of the APA journals is *Webster's* (25), and all problems of preferred spelling and the like should be referred to it.

4.1 *Capitalization*

Rules for capitalization are extensive, and general references (20, 22, 23) should be consulted. Only three problems often met in psychological journals are taken up here.

4.11 *Titles of books.* The exact title of a book has every main word capitalized when printed in the body of an article, and is also underlined to show italics. In the reference list, only the initial letter of the first word is capitalized (see sec. 8.82).

4.12 *Titles of tests, etc.* When the words *test, scale, schedule, inventory,* and the like are used in a generic sense, they are not capitalized. When they are a part of the exact title of a particular test or form, capitalization is used. Hence we have the Porteus Maze Test, the Wechsler Adult Intelligence Scale, the Strong Vocational Interest Blank, and the Minnesota Multiphasic Personality Inventory. Sometimes inexact words are used in naming an instrument. These are not capitalized: the Rorschach test (but, the Rorschach Psychodiagnostic), and the Wechsler test (but, the Wechsler Adult Intelligence Scale).

4.13 *Institutions and persons.* Do not capitalize departments (as department of psychology) unless used as an address, or titles unless they precede a name. It is Professor Charles A. Lincoln, Department of Psychology, Englewood University, but Charles A. Lincoln, professor of psychology in Englewood University. The names of specific schools are capitalized, as Duke University, or the Medical School (when referring to a particular one), but are not capitalized when used generically, as in the phrase *accredited medical schools.*

4.2 Compound Words

In English, compound words may be written in various instances as (*a*) combined unbroken words, (*b*) hyphenated words, or (*c*) separate words. Modern practice, generally adopted by APA journals, favors the combined unhyphenated forms. For a full discussion, see the reference manuals (**20, 22, 23**). On particular words, consult Webster's (**25**), which generally shows whether to use the unbroken or hyphenated form. Only a few cases of special interest to psychological journals can be cited here.

4.21 *Words formed with prefixes.* Words formed with prefixes— *bi, co, non, over, pre, sub,* and the like—usually do not require a hyphen. A general rule is to omit the hyphen unless the word is "unusual." Since technical journals use many words that would be "unusual" in newspapers and popular books but which are quite familiar to persons in a profession, they tend to use fewer hyphens. Here are a few examples of words that are not hyphenated in technical writing:

bipolar	postencephalitic
coeducation	posttest
nondirective	pretest
nonschizophrenic	reunite
overaggressive	subtest

Some *exceptions* which require the use of a hyphen are:

a. When necessary to avoid confusion of meaning: *re-pair* (to pair again).

b. When the vowels would form a diphthong or suggest mispronunciation: *co-author, co-worker.*

c. When the word to which the prefix is added is a proper name: *non-Freudian.*

d. When the word begins with the terminal vowel of the prefix: *re-examine.*

But, an exception to an exception is the writing of *coordinate* and *cooperate,* and all their variant forms, without the hyphen. These words are used frequently, and the hyphen destroys the sense of unity essential to their meanings. An especially awkward form is "unco-ordinated"; *uncoordinated* is preferred.

4.22 *Do not use prefixes as words.* A prefix, which is intended to be joined to a word with or without a hyphen, may never stand alone as if it were a word. Examples:

Incorrect: . . . the non schizophrenic subjects . . . .
Correct: . . . the nonschizophrenic subjects . . . .
Incorrect: . . . the differences between the tests given pre and post.
Correct: . . . the differences between the pretests and the posttests.
Still better: . . . the differences between the tests given before and after the training.

4.23 *Some other compounds.* Compounds of an adjective and a noun, or of two nouns, often fuse together with frequent use. Thus we use no hyphens in *casework, classroom, feebleminded, formboard, textbook,* and *workshop.* Long technical phrases are best written as separate words without hyphens: *child welfare research, public health administration,* etc.

4.3 *Use of Italics*

When you underline a word in a manuscript, you are instructing the printer to set that word in italics. Italics should be used sparingly.

4.31 *Italics required.* Titles of published books and names of journals when used in running text should always be italicized and also capitalized.

Unassimilated foreign words are italicized; common and well-assimilated foreign words are not. It is unnecessary to provide a list because *Webster's* (**25**) indicates by a special symbol—two vertical lines in front of the word—the words and phrases of foreign origin that should be italicized; others found in *Webster's* should not be italicized. The Chicago *Manual* (**23**) discusses use of italics at length.

4.32 *Italics permitted.* When a new and important term is introduced, or when a key word early in a paragraph is stressed in lieu of a heading, the word may be italicized. This practice serves as a supplementary method of outlining.

When the meaning or use of a word is being discussed, it is appropriate to set if off by means of italics. Example: The word *test* is capitalized only when . . . .

4.33 *Italics discouraged.* In technical writing, italics should rarely be used for emphasis. An occasional *not,* where needed, should be the limit. Excessive use of italics for emphasis, imitating the stresses that can be made in oral speech, characterizes an immature style of writing. Give stress by headings, by paragraphing, and by the structure of sentences. Do not underline long phrases or whole sentences to give them prominence.

4.4 *Punctuation*

Punctuation is a complex topic, and standard references should be consulted (**20, 22, 23**). A few points that seem to give trouble in psychological writing are:

4.41 *Commas.* Technical writing should be "tight," and it is best to use commas freely. In an enumeration of three or more items, use a comma before the *and:* " . . . the height, width, and depth . . . ."

There is often confusion as to whether a clause should be set off by commas. A *defining* clause, which limits the meaning of the word it modifies, does not use commas. (Example: " . . . the switch that stops the recording device.") A *nondefining* clause, not limiting the meaning, is set off by commas. (Example: " . . . the switch, which is placed on a panel, controls . . . .")

4.42 *Hyphens.* The hyphen, even aside from its use in compound words, is a demon among punctuation marks. Perhaps a few examples will help.

a. A compound modifier is hyphenated when ambiguity may be avoided thereby:
. . . characteristic of client-centered counseling . . . .
. . . exceeded the control-group mean . . . .
b. The same word groups, however, are not hyphenated when they do not constitute a modifier:
. . . the counseling is client centered . . . .
. . . used a control group . . . .
c. When two or more compound words have a common base, the base may be indicated in all but the last by a hyphen. Note the space following the first hyphen in the illustrations.
a fourth- or fifth-grade class
two- and three-year-olds
the pre- and posttests
d. Fractional expressions use the hyphen:
one-half; four and five-sevenths; half-asleep
e. The compounds of *self-* are usually hyphenated: *self-conscious, self-evident.* But the phrase *the self concept,* i.e., the concept of the self, is not hyphenated.

4.43 *Dash.* In typescript, the dash is always indicated by two hyphens, not one. Do not leave a typewriter space before or after the hyphens or between them.

4.44 *Quotation marks.* In American practice, double quotation marks are used to indicate primary quotations, whether of a single word, or of one or two sentences. There is a common misconception that a single word is placed in single quotation marks. Not so! Example: The so-called "nervous" rats . . . .

Quotations within a quotation are enclosed in single quotation marks if the whole quotation is in double quotation marks. Example: The experimenter reported, "When I said, 'Ready, go,' in a loud voice, the subject was startled."

When a quotation is set off from the text in reduced type (see sec. 4.74), quotations within it are enclosed in double quotation marks.

In American typographic practice, it is universally accepted that the period and the comma are *always* placed before the closing quotation mark, even when the quotation marks enclose only a single word.

25

Failure to follow this rule results in costly copy editing or proof correction. Examples: The subjects were "nervous," even between trials. "He repeated, 'Think, think.'" Colons and semicolons are always placed after the quotation mark. An interrogation point is placed after the quotation mark, unless the question is itself part of the quoted material.

Contemporary Psychology uses both double and single quotation marks distinguished as follows. Double quotes are used when the quoted material is specific as to time and place if uttered, or as to place if printed. Single quotes are used for looser approximate quotations, or when a word or phrase is used about which the writer is apologetic or humorous. Examples: Smith refers to the behavior as "deviant." (The reviewer is quoting a word exactly as used in the book.) Occasionally Jones becomes a bit 'preachy.' (The reviewer is indicating an apology for using a word which he does not like, but which expresses a conventional meaning.)

4.45 *Parentheses.* One set of parentheses is never enclosed within another. Brackets are used in place of parentheses within parentheses. Example: (For a further discussion, see the *Manual of Style* [23, p. 111].)

4.5 *Numbers*

Numbers less than ten are ordinarily spelled out. Write " . . . used three [not 3] groups . . . ." However, there are several specific exceptions:

Numbers less than ten are given as numerals when they come in a series such as 3, 8, 11, and 17; indicate a page in a bibliographic reference; are comparable to two-digit numbers used in the same paragraph; express scores or percentages; or precede an abbreviation indicating quantity, such as *3 ft.*

Exact numbers of more than one digit are given in arabic numerals; round numbers are usually spelled out.

Never begin a sentence with a numeral, even if other numbers follow. For example, you must write: "Forty-three men and 38 women replied." Usually it is better to recast such sentences, as: "Replies were received from 43 men and 38 women."

4.6 *Abbreviations and Symbols*

4.61 *Abbreviations.* In scientific writing, abbreviations are used for many technical and statistical terms. A sentence, however, never begins with an abbreviation. Very helpful lists of abbreviations of psychological terms and of units of measurement frequently used by psychologists are given by Daniel and Louttit (**9**, pp. 386–398). For a discussion of abbreviations and for lists of commonly used general abbreviations, see the references on style (**20, 22, 23**).

a. Abbreviations for many widely understood psychological terms are typewritten in all capital letters without spaces or periods between them. They do not need to be explained. Examples: CA, MA, IQ, EQ, PR.

b. Longer technical terms and names of techniques, if they occur frequently in a particular paper, are spelled out when first used and followed by their abbreviations in parentheses. Thereafter, only the abbreviation is used. For example, an author refers to the electroencephalogram (EEG), or to the Thematic Apperception Test (TAT). The abbreviations consist of all capital letters without spaces or periods. Some other common examples are: AGCT, EKG, MMPI, PGR, and WISC.

c. Names of familiar general, scientific, and government organizations, and military terms, are abbreviated in capital letters without spaces or periods. Examples: AAAS, APA, NRC, SPSSI, SSRC, USAF, USN, VA, and YMCA.

4.62 *Abbreviation of experimenter, subject, etc.* In APA journals, the word *experimenter* is often abbreviated *E; subject, S;* and *observer, O.* Care must be taken to distinguish between the plural forms of these abbreviations, which add the letter s without an apostrophe, and the possessive forms which use an apostrophe. Examples:

E experimenter	*S* subject
Es experimenters	*Ss* subjects
E's experimenter's	*S's* subject's
Es' experimenters'	*Ss'* subjects'

In typing these abbreviations, the capital letters *E, S,* and *O* are underlined to indicate italics, but the small letter s which shows plural or possessive form is *not* underlined and is printed in roman type.

4.63 *Per cent and percentage.* Either the words *per cent* or the per cent sign, *%,* may be used to indicate percentage quantities in the text of articles in APA journals. Each author should be consistent within a manuscript. When *per cent* is spelled out, it is written as two words.

For economy, the % sign is always used with conventional Rorschach symbols, as *A%, F+%,* etc.

Good usage requires that the term *per cent* or the % sign be preceded by a number. The word *percentage* is used when a number is not given. Examples: " . . . found that 18% [or 18 per cent] of the subjects . . . ." " . . . determined the percentage of subjects that . . . ."

4.64 *Symbols.* Letters used as statistical symbols should ordinarily follow standard American practice, as defined by Dunlap and Kurtz

(10), Kurtz and Edgerton (15), and most textbooks on statistics. Letters with bars, wavy lines, or dots above or below them should be avoided unless the author believes them essential. They cause the printer trouble, and therefore add to expense. Greek letters, and subscript and superscript letters may be used.

4.65 *Typing symbols.* Letters used as symbols for statistical concepts, and also for certain conventional test scores, are italicized in print and therefore must be underlined in the manuscript. Do *not* enclose such symbols in quotation marks. Examples: t, N, df [degrees of freedom], an F ratio, a T score, a Q sort; the W, d, or $F\%$ of the Rorschach; the Hs and Pd scales of the MMPI.

Do not join such a symbol to the following related word with a hyphen, unless the symbol and word constitute a modifier. (The principle is the same as that stated in sec. 4.42*a*, *b*.) Examples: The t test (*not* t-test) showed .... A Q sort (*not* Q-sort) was made ... ; *but:* The study used the Q-sort technique.

Special symbols, such as those used in Hull's behavior theory, should be carefully hand printed, without crowding, so as to be optimally legible to the editor and printer.

4.66 *Formulas.* Because statistical and other mathematical formulas are expensive to set in type, they should not be given unless new or rare, and essential to the author's argument. Common statistical procedures should be used without explanation or reference. Less common formulas and procedures should be accompanied by a reference to a book or article in which they may be found.

Unless an essential statistical formula can readily be introduced into a single line of typewriting (e.g., if it has no fraction signs or complex exponents), it should be placed on a widely spaced line by itself. If the formula is too complex to be typed clearly, it should be carefully lettered by hand. Pay special attention to the clear alignment of fractions, exponents, and subscripts.

4.7 *References and Quotations in the Text*

4.71 *References.* Show all references in the text by numbers in parentheses that refer to the list of references at the end of the article. The reference numbers may be used with or without authors' names. Examples: "Manuals on editorial style (20, 22, 23) advise that ...." "Fowler (12) gives amusing examples ...."

a. Several reference numbers cited at the same point are given in numerical order, separated by commas, and enclosed in one pair of parentheses. A space follows each comma.

b. To refer to a particular page, pages, or chapter of a reference, give the citation in the parentheses, following the reference number. Examples: (1, p. 410), (23, pp. 150–153), (11, ch. 2).

c. When reference is made to one source in general, and to particular pages of another source, use a semicolon to separate the reference numbers. Example: (**12**; **20**, pp. 402–522).

d. Do not use footnotes to cite references to the literature. Cite the reference by number, and give the full description in the alphabetical list at the end of the article.

4.72 *Quotations.* Quotations should be given exactly as they appear in the source. The original wording, punctuation, spelling, italics, etc. must be preserved even if they are erroneous. Authors should routinely check the typed copy of quotations with the original source before submitting their manuscripts.

4.73 *Short quotations.* A short quotation of a sentence or two, which would not be more than five lines when printed, is incorporated in the text, and is set off by quotation marks.

4.74 *Longer quotations.* Longer quotations, of more than five printed lines, are printed in smaller type. When making a longer quotation: begin a new paragraph; double space between each and every line; do not give an additional indention to every line; do not use quotation marks (see sec. 3.41). To indicate to the editor that such a passage is a quotation, draw a light vertical pencil line in the left margin, extending from the first line of the quotation to the last.

4.75 *Additions to and deletions from quotations.* Any material inserted in a quotation by the author of an article is enclosed in brackets.

If words are omitted from a quotation, three spaced periods (called an *ellipsis*) are inserted. If the omitted words appear after a complete sentence or complete a sentence, there will be four periods rather than three.

4.76 *Reference to quotation.* The citation of the source of a direct quotation should always include the page or pages as well as the reference number. The citation is given in parentheses, following the last word of the quoted material. It precedes the final period of the quotation, but is not within the quotation marks when quotation marks are used.

4.8 *Footnotes*

The use of footnotes should be minimized. Avoid the temptation to bring in questionably relevant material or parenthetical discussions by using footnotes. Generally, such content should be omitted. When clearly pertinent, it can usually be integrated with the text.

4.81 *Numbering footnotes.* Footnotes to the text, including those attached to the title and to authors' names, should be numbered consecutively throughout the article or monograph with superscript arabic numerals. Do not use asterisks, etc. (For footnotes to tables, see sec. 5.8.)

4.82 *Place of footnotes.* Text footnotes should be typed with double spacing on a separate page placed at the end of the manuscript (see sec. 9.2). Several footnotes may be typed on such a page; a separate page for each footnote is *not* required. Each footnote should begin with a paragraph indention, and with its superscript reference number. Remember to double space between each and every line.

4.9 *Appendixes*

An appendix has no place in a journal article. Material thought suitable for appendixes should be deleted, integrated with the text in abbreviated form, placed in a table, or, perhaps best, be given auxiliary publication (see sec. 6).

Appendixes may be appropriate in *Psychological Monographs,* and are placed after the text and before the references.

5. *Tabular Presentation*

Good tabular presentation sets forth quantitative data systematically, precisely, and economically, by the skillful combination of the elements of a table. Effective tabular presentation facilitates comparisons both within the table and among the tables.

5.01 *References on tabular presentation.* Worth-while references on tables include the comprehensive manual for the U. S. Bureau of the Census by Jenkinson (14), and the manual of the Social Security Board (21). Walker and Durost (24), although now old, is specifically oriented toward statistical presentations in education and psychology, and includes a chapter on the analysis and criticism of tables.

5.02 *Terminology.* In order to discuss tables, it is necessary to refer to the technical names of their elements or parts. The principal parts of a moderately complex, single-page table are named in Fig. 1. The reader should refer to the figure frequently while studying the sections below.

5.1 *Economy in Tabular Presentation*

The printing of tables, even from the best-prepared copy, is expensive. Hence it is necessary to keep tabular material to a minimum con-

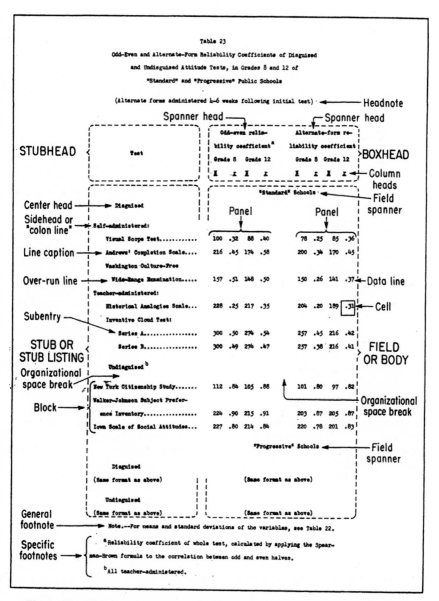

Fig. 1. Identification of the major parts of a table. The illustration also provides an example of the arrangement, spacing, and alignment of a well-prepared typewritten table. Note that overrun lines are indented two spaces; subentries are indented four spaces.

sistent with reasonably adequate presentation. The following recommendations should be observed.

5.11 *Do not tabulate original data.* Original data—test scores, ratings, protocols—should rarely be submitted for journal publication, but deserve auxiliary publication in some instances (see sec. 6).

5.12 *Prepare tables in condensed form.* Statistical data should be presented in the most highly condensed form that permits communication.

a. Original and intermediate compilations and calculations should rarely be shown.

b. A complete tabular presentation of statistical results is not always necessary. It may be sufficient to present the average and range of the correlations between judges' ratings, for example, instead of a table of correlations between each pair of judges. Similarly, it may be best to present full data on the matching of two subgroups with respect to one principal variable instead of with respect to several variables, especially if the variables are known to be intercorrelated.

c. Extensive tables of nonsignificant results are seldom required. For example, if only 2 of 20 correlations are significantly different from zero, the 2 significant correlations may be mentioned in the text, and the rest dismissed with a few words.

5.13 *Prime and nonprime data.* The distinction between *prime* (independent) and *nonprime* (dependent) data often suggests a means for reducing the size of a table.

In a table giving the results of an analysis of variance and covariance, one column was devoted to *Sum of squares* and the adjoining column to *Mean square* (variance). Inasmuch as the *Sum of squares* is an intermediate figure, and recoverable from the data presented on *Mean square* and *df* (degrees of freedom), the *Sum of squares* could be eliminated without loss.

A similar redundancy occurs when one column is devoted to *p* (probability of chance occurrence) and the next column to a verbal statement that the hypothesis is "accepted" or "rejected." Since the latter depends wholly on *p*, it may be eliminated in favor of a statement in the text or in a table footnote that no hypothesis is accepted unless *p* falls below some specified value.

In a few instances, reader convenience requires that nonprime data be included. Thus, in a study in which sex differences are of substantial but secondary interest, it would be helpful to present means for men, for women, and for the total group.

5.14 *Avoid repetition of data.* Ordinarily, an identical column of figures should not appear in two tables. When two tables overlap, consideration should be given to the feasibility of combining them into one. Occasionally, however, reader convenience justifies some overlap.

No column or row of a table should be retained which carries the same entry throughout. If the number of cases, *N*, is identical for each of several groups, do not have a column for *N*, but supply the information in a headnote (sec. 5.33) or table footnote (sec. 5.8).

A row or column of a table which contains few entries can usually be eliminated. The few entries may be supplied in a table footnote.

5.15 *Significant figures.* For economy, as well as for statistical precision, do not express quantities in tables to a number of digits beyond their significance. Consult statistics textbooks for discussions of significant figures. A common error, for example, is to express means and standard deviations to four or five digits when only two or three places are significant. Two decimal places suffice for correlation coefficients in almost all instances.

5.2 General Mechanics of Presentation

5.21 *Type each table on a separate sheet.* Each table, no matter how short, should be typed on a separate sheet. In printing, the compositor who sets tables is generally not the one who sets the text.

5.22 *Type number and title centered.* The word *Table* and the arabic number of the table should be centered at the top of the page. The table title, also centered on the page, should begin two spaces below the table number. If the title requires two or more lines, it should be double spaced, and each line should be centered. Capitalize only the initial letters of principal words; do not use a terminal period. See Fig. 1 for an example.

5.23 *Use wide spacing.* Always double space every part of a table—the title, the headnote, the headings, the stub, the data lines, and the footnotes. If possible, triple space above and below column headings, to give the editor space to add rulings.

Narrower spacing—space-and-a-half or, reluctantly, single spacing —is permissible only if necessary to confine the table to a single sheet, but a two-page typewritten table is preferable to a crowded single-page one.

5.24 *Rule completely with light pencil lines.* Rule your table completely, including both horizontal and vertical rules, with *light* pencil lines, which will not appear in the printed version. The purpose of the light ruling is to insure clarity. A well-prepared table is easy to rule; a poor one cannot be ruled successfully. If you cannot rule your table without cutting into typewritten material, redraft the table. In Fig. 1, the light ruling is not shown, to avoid overcrowding.

5.25 *Make no heavy rules.* Make *no* heavy rules on the table, either horizontal or vertical. The editor will add the conventional heavy rules when he prepares the table for the printer.

5.26 *Indicate position of table.* In the typescript, indicate by a brief note where a table is to appear, thus:

```
---------------------------------------------------------------
                    Insert Table 1 about here
---------------------------------------------------------------
```

5.27 *Refer to tables by number.* In the text, always refer to tables by their numbers. Refer to "Table 1" and "Table 2," not to "the following table," or the table "above" or "below." For reasons of layout, the printer usually cannot place the table exactly in the position suggested. Also avoid reference to "the table on page . . . " since the printed page number cannot be known until after page proof has been run, and the insertion of a page number at that stage is expensive.

5.3 Table Headings

Every tabular presentation should be given a table number and title. *Never* use a "headless table" introduced by a sentence such as "These facts are shown by the table below."

5.31 *Table number.* Tables are numbered in arabic (*not* roman) numerals, consecutively from the beginning of the article or monograph to the end, including the tables in an appendix of a monograph. Avoid the use of suffix letters to indicate a relationship between successive tables; do not refer to Tables 5, 5A, and 5B, but to Tables 5, 6, and 7. Type the table number centered on the page. For the designation of tables to be deposited with the ADI, see sec. 6.21.

5.32 *Table title.* Every table has a title which should be brief but clear and distinctive. The title should generally be prepared after the table itself has been drafted, yet be oriented to the reader who of course looks at the title first. Use a "telegraphic" style of writing. Do not attempt a complete inventory of the table's contents. Maintain stylistic consistency between the various table titles in the report.

The table subtitle, if any, should be centered below the title. Capitalize only the first letter of each main word.

5.33 *Table headnote.* A headnote is a general note at the top of a table, under the title or subtitle. A headnote qualifies, explains, or provides information relating to the table as a whole. Thus, the headnote may contain a statement of N, may point out a specific exclusion from the table, etc. Do not use a headnote for general discussion, which belongs in the text.

Type a headnote double spaced, and enclosed in parentheses, with only the initial letter of its first word capitalized.

5.4 *Stubhead and Stub*

5.41 *Stubhead.* (See Fig. 1.) The stubhead serves to classify or describe the principal line captions of the stub. Always use a stubhead; if the stub listings are very heterogeneous, *Item* may be used. Type the stubhead centered in the stub box, with only its first letter capitalized.

5.42 *Phrasing in the stub.* Line captions should be phrased as specifically as limitations of space permit. Captions such as *All groups, Both sexes, All trials*, etc. are preferable to *Total.* It is also essential that line captions, especially those under a center or side heading, be phrased in uniform or comparable fashion. Thus line captions under a heading *Behavior problem* should be uniformly nouns, or verbs, or verbal nouns, etc. Preferred: *truancy, nailbiting, overaggressiveness*, etc., rather than a miscellany such as *truancy, bites fingernails, very aggressive*, etc.

5.43 *Format of stub.* Subordination in the stub is shown by *center heads* and *sideheads*, as illustrated in Fig. 1. Common errors are to place headings in an additional column at the left, or to run them vertically at the left; such practices waste space and must be avoided.

Line captions should be arranged to facilitate comparisons within a table and between tables. Insofar as possible, lines to be compared should be placed in analogous positions in the blocks.

In typing the stub, *never* type any word in all capital letters or underline any word. Other desirable aspects of format are shown in Fig. 1. Note that line captions following a sidehead are indented four typewriter spaces. Over-run lines are given a hanging indention of two typewriter spaces.

5.44 *Nonhomogeneous material.* A line caption or group of line captions not homogeneous with the remaining captions of the stub—e.g., a *Total* or a *Mean* following a series of detailed line captions—may have its special nature indicated by extra indention, by extra vertical spacing above and below, or by both.

5.5 *Boxhead*

The basic unit of the boxhead is the *column head* or heading of the individual column. A heading which spans two or more column heads is a *spanner* or *spanner head*. A higher order or superior spanner subsumes two or more lower spanners. In general, no more than two levels of spanner heads are desirable, although occasionally another level may be necessary (see Fig. 1).

5.51 *Position and spacing.* Each column head must be centered exactly over the column of entries to which it refers. Similarly, each spanner must be centered exactly over the column heads, or lower-order spanners, to which it refers. Generous space—preferably a triple space—should be allowed above and below each column head and spanner to permit the editor to insert horizontal rules without crowding. These directions must be followed exactly if errors and the expensive resetting of tables are to be avoided.

5.52 *Format of boxhead.* Column and spanner heads should be typed in small letters, with only the initial letter of the first word capitalized, without a terminal period. If a spanner head is "read into" the column heads below—the spanner and each column head forming a continuous phrase—a terminal dash is employed.

The headings should all be typed horizontally on the page, except in very unusual circumstances. If the headings are unavoidably too long, they may be typed vertically. If typed vertically, headings read up, never down.

5.53 *Phrasing in the boxhead.* Column heads should be phrased in uniform or comparable fashion (see sec. 5.42).

Column heads and spanners are generally expressed in the singular: *Age* (not Ages), *Mean* (not Means), *Mean salary* (not Mean salaries). However, if each entry applies to a group, the plural form is appropriate: *Men, Teachers colleges, Trials 1–4,* etc. Similarly, units are expressed in the plural: *Seconds, Years of service,* etc. Because of space limitations, brief phrasing, telegraphic style, and appropriate abbreviations are used in the boxhead. Brevity, unfortunately, can lead to ambiguity.

When complete clarity is impossible within the boxhead, consideration should be given to such devices as: (*a*) transposing from boxhead to stub, where more space is generally available, (*b*) adding one or more appropriate footnotes, or (*c*) making use of symbols or code letters, explained in a headnote or in footnotes—a device to be used only as a last resort.

5.54 *Arrangement.* Columns should be arranged so as to facilitate desired comparisons. Insofar as possible, comparison columns should be adjacent. Comparison columns in different panels of the table should be placed in comparable positions within the panels.

5.6 *Field or Body of the Table*

5.61 *Field entries.* Principally, the field or body of a table contains the numerical data, which may be regarded as *column entries* in the vertical aspect, as *data lines* in the horizontal aspect, or as *cell entries* in the twofold aspect. A *cell* is the space common to a column and a row.

5.62 *Spacing within the table.* The purpose of spacing between lines is either to make more explicit the organization of the table, or to make the reading of the table perceptually easier. Occasionally, spacing between lines may be used (*a*) to separate a relatively nonhomogeneous line or group of lines from a preceding homogeneous group, or (*b*) to separate one group or block of data from another.

Related columns of data may be set off in panels by means of spacing between appropriate columns. Shortage of space, however, commonly limits extensive use of this device.

5.63 *Field spanners.* A field spanner (see Fig. 1) is a spanner set in the body of a table to indicate its organization. Note that the first field spanner is set *below* the boxhead, never above it, and that field spanners are limited to the *field* of the table and never project into the *stub*.

5.7 The Size of a Table

5.71 *The dimensions of a table.* The *width* of a table is determined, in general, by (*a*) the number of "characters" in the longest lines of the stub and the columns of the table, (*b*) the spacing between columns, also measured in "characters," and (*c*) the size of type used. A "character" is any letter, number, punctuation mark, or unit of horizontal space. Not all "characters" require the same amount of space in printing—an *i* requires less space than an *m*—but this fact does not require consideration save in the tightest of tables.

The *depth* of a table is determined by (*a*) its number of lines from the first line of the table heading to the last line of the footnotes, (*b*) the spacing between lines, and (*c*) the size of the type.

5.72 *Maximum sizes of tables in APA journals.* Table 1 reports the maximum page capacities in 1957 of the APA journals which print tabular material. It must be emphasized that these are maximum figures, and that tables approaching these sizes will appear dense and crowded. It is best to plan tables well within the stated capacities. Insofar as possible, authors should plan to use single-column tables, unless full-page width is clearly required. Broadside tables, printed at right angles to the usual page arrangement, and multipage tables should be used only rarely.

An author should count the characters and spaces in each typewritten table so as to avoid submitting a table just a little too large for the intended position in the article. A thoughtful rearrangement, or the omission of a superfluous column (see sec. 5.1), may adapt a table to fit the space available.

5.73 *Planning a table.* Tables that are too long in one dimension and too short in the other are inefficient and unattractive.

Table 1

Capacity of Tabular Pages in Journals of the American
Psychological Association Which Print Tables: 1957

Journal	Upright			Broadside	
	No. of characters per line		No. of lines on pages	No. of characters per line	No. of lines on page
	Single column of double-column page	Full page			
American Psychologist					
8-point type	54	112	77	154	56
6-point type	72	148	102	204	74
Journal of Abnormal and Social Psychology					
8-point type	48	99	72	144	50
6-point type	64	132	96	192	66
Journal of Applied Psychology					
8-point type	48	99	72	144	50
6-point type	64	132	96	192	66
Journal of Comparative and Physiological Psychology					
8-point type	48	99	72	144	50
6-point type	64	132	96	192	66
Journal of Consulting Psychology					
8-point type	48	99	72	144	50
6-point type	64	132	96	192	66
Journal of Experimental Psychology					
8-point type	42	88	68	136	44
6-point type	56	116	90	180	58
Psychological Bulletin					
8-point type	42	88	68	136	44
6-point type	56	116	90	180	58
Psychological Monographs					
8-point type	45	94	69	138	47
6-point type	60	124	92	184	62
Psychological Review					
8-point type	42	88	68	136	44
6-point type	56	116	90	180	58

Note.—The unit of the "character" reported in the table is the printer's *en*, which equals one-half an *em*. A sufficiently accurate estimate can usually be obtained by counting each typewritten character *and space* as one "unit." When greater precision is required, the following measures may be used:
½ unit: i j l , . ; : ' -
1 unit: a b c d e f f fi fl g h k n o p q r s t u v x y z " - I J
1½ units: fi ffl m w A B C D E F G H K L N O P Q R S T U V X Y Z
2 units: M W —
Small capitals are the same as lower case except L is 1 unit. Numerals are all 1 unit.

To avoid *pencil-like tables*—lengthy stub, narrow boxhead—it is sometimes helpful to use a *double section* arrangement. The stub, instead of appearing as a single column, is divided into two columns, the second stub column appearing in the right-hand half of the table. In this case, the boxhead is repeated in the second section. For an illustration, see Jenkinson (14, p. 14).

To avoid *ribbon-like tables*—short stub, wide boxhead—use should be made of expedients such as (*a*) rearrangement to incorporate some elements of the boxhead into the stub, or (*b*) the use of a *double deck* arrangement, in which the boxhead is cut in two, the second half appearing as a lower "deck" below the first half. In this case, the stub is repeated in the lower deck. For an illustration, see Jenkinson (14, p. 17).

5.8 *Table Footnotes*

5.81 *Phrasing and format.* The brief footnotes appropriate to tables are phrased in "telegraphic" style. When the subject of a verb is omitted, the singular form of the verb is used:

[a] Includes 30 cases for whom data. . . .

Each footnote to a table should begin with a paragraph indention. Footnotes are typed double spaced, or at least with space-and-a-half separation, across the full width of the page immediately below the table.

5.82 *Reference symbols to table footnotes.* General footnotes which pertain to a table as a whole are typed immediately below the table and are preceded by the word *Note* which is followed by a period and a dash.

Specific footnotes, which refer to the stub or to particular column headings, line captions, or cell entries follow in order. The reference marks should be superscript small letters, [a,b,c...] used in order, with the footnotes arranged alphabetically by their superscripts. The footnotes of a table are independent of those of any other table and of the text, and begin with [a] in each table. When the same footnote pertains to more than one referent, the same reference letter is placed after each such referent. Note that the asterisk, etc., is *no longer used* to indicate the specific footnotes to tables.

The asterisk (*) and double asterisk (**) may be used only for the special case of indicating the probability level of tests of significance. When two levels of significance are footnoted, the lower level (e.g., .05 or .01) should be given a single asterisk, and the higher level (e.g., .01 or .001) should be given two asterisks. If more than two levels of significance are noted, the letters [a,b,c] should be used. Examples:

* Significant at .05 level.
** Significant at .01 level.

5.83 *Continuation of multipage tables.* It is well to add a continuation footnote to the bottom of every page but the last of a multipage table. Such a footnote is unlettered, centered, in parentheses, and placed below all other footnotes, as follows: (Table continued on next page).

6. *Auxiliary Publication*

Auxiliary publication is a resource for making available materials that cannot economically be included in a printed article or monograph. Materials appropriate for auxiliary publication may include protocols or original observations, tabulations of original data, tables giving complete detailed data (frequency distributions, detailed findings for numerous subsamples, intermediate matrices of factor analyses, etc.), detailed drawings of apparatus, large-sized charts, and photographs (including color photographs).

The essential steps of auxiliary publication are (*a*) to place the materials where they will be available to interested specialists, and (*b*) to publish a notice of their availability.

6.1 *Local Auxiliary Publication Resources*

6.12 *Private reproduction not desirable.* To reproduce materials privately is usually not feasible because of the expense involved. Nor is it desirable, because there is no assurance that the materials will be available to scholars at a later date. Therefore, editors generally discourage the insertion of footnotes in articles stating that further materials are available from the authors.

The *Journal of Consulting Psychology* allows such footnotes to indicate where to secure a more extended account of the studies published as Brief Reports, but the extended report is also filed with the ADI to insure its availability.

6.13 *Library publication.* Materials may be deposited in university or other libraries which are willing and able to undertake interlibrary loans or to provide photostat or microfilm copies. Masters' theses and doctors' dissertations are ordinarily so deposited.

The reference to deposited materials, when given in an article, should include the author's name, the exact title, the name and location of the library, and the exact page numbers on which the materials in question may be found, to permit the library quickly and without error to make the photostat or microfilm copies.

6.2 *American Documentation Institute*

The best resource for auxiliary publication is the American Documentation Institute (ADI), now operated as a service of the Library of Congress.

6.21 *Preparation of materials for the ADI.* Materials for transmission to the ADI should be adapted to photographic processes. A white background is best. Drawings should be in jet black ink. Photographs should have good contrast. Typewritten materials should be sharply defined, not faint or blurred. Carbon or pencil copies are undesirable for several reasons. Blue ink is quite inappropriate because it will not photograph. Typewritten materials may be single spaced for economy but should not be crowded. Pages of standard typewriter size are preferred for filing, but other sizes are received when essential. The name, institutional connection, and permanent address of the author should appear conspicuously on the material.

Tables to be deposited with the ADI are designated as Table A, Table B, etc., and figures as Figure A, Figure B, etc. The text of the article may refer to them by using these letters as identification. Referring to such tables and figures by letters distinguishes them from those printed in the article, which are numbered with arabic numerals.

6.22 *Notice of availability.* The ADI accepts materials to which reference is made in an article published for general circulation. The author should include a notice of availability in his manuscript, usually in the form of a footnote reading substantially as follows:

[1] A 5-page table giving data for each of the subgroups [or other described material] has been deposited with the American Documentation Institute. Order Document No.——, remitting $—— for 35-mm. microfilm or $—— for 6 by 8 in. photocopies.

The managing editor adds the document number and prices to the footnote when the information has been supplied by the ADI.

6.23 *Send ADI materials to the journal editor.* Materials to be deposited with the ADI in connection with an article should always be sent to the journal editor with the manuscript. The editor needs to see them when judging the acceptability of the article. Editors have arrangements to deposit materials with the ADI through the APA Central Office.

7. *Preparation of Figures*

Graphs are the most economical and intelligible mode of presentation for certain types of data. But graphs, charts, and photographs are expensive both to the author and to the APA. Also their design and preparation seem to cause considerable difficulty to many authors. The author should therefore ask with respect to every graph or photograph presented for publication: Is this figure necessary? Is it economical of journal space? Is it prepared with quality suitable for publication?

It is highly recommended that authors secure the services of a professional draftsman, if possible. Most psychologists do not have the technical skill required to produce a satisfactory figure.

7.01 *References on graphic presentation.* The most complete and detailed sources for the principles, layout, and drawing of figures are two pamphlets issued by the American Standards Association (2, 3). They contain illustrations of good and bad practices. Some statistics textbooks contain sections on graphic methods, and there are several extensive texts or manuals (4, 7, 13, 26).

7.1 *Subject Matter Suitable for Figures*

Some subject matter is particularly suitable for graphic representation. Graphs are especially well adapted to displaying changes of functions and rates of change. They are helpful in clarifying comparisons between different individuals or groups, and between successive measures of the same groups or individuals. Therefore, graphs are appropriate for showing learning curves, extinction curves, changes with age, changes in performance under systematically varying conditions, frequency polygons of the performance of contrasting groups, and test profiles of individuals or groups.

Unnecessary or inappropriate graphs are illustrated by: scatter-plots for correlations' when the linearity of the regression line is not in question or the subject of discussion; photographs of apparatus, when the photograph reveals little that cannot be adequately described by a word picture or by a line drawing of critical parts; a plot of the relationship between two or more variables, when the relationship is simple (i.e., linear), when the number of points plotted is not more than two, or when the text does not stress a comparison of curve slopes or curve forms.

7.2 *Size and Proportion of Figures*

· 7.21 *Relationship to page size.* The size of an efficient figure bears a definite relationship to the size of the journal's page, and especially to the width of the column of type. Perhaps the most common and wasteful error in the preparation of a graph or a chart is to draw it without reference to the page size and format of the journal in which it is to be published. As a consequence, the editor must publish it as a two-column figure in order to have proper readability of the legends or discriminability of the graph points, even though there is much white space on both sides of the graph. In many cases, a simple adjustment of the ratio of vertical and horizontal axes, or larger lettering, would have permitted its presentation as a one-column figure with a saving of up to 75 per cent in the page space required.

7.22 *Planning the figure.* After making a rough sketch of the content of his figure, the author's first task is to design it to fit the journal page.

He should measure the one-column and full-page widths of the journal of his choice, and examine good examples of one-column and two-column figures of the type he plans to use. A decision is then reached as to whether the figure can be made to fit one column, or if it must be two.

The drawing area should then be made about two linear times the size planned for the printed figure. In computing the space to be filled by the drawing when printed, allowance should be made for the legends for the vertical and horizontal axes. It is not necessary to restrict the figure size to integral values, for each rectangle constructed on an extension of the diagonal of the desired printed size will preserve the same proportion in the reduction (see Fig. 2).

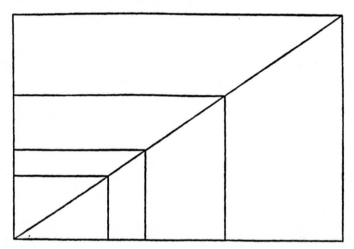

Fig. 2. Enlarging a figure in proportion. Any rectangle constructed on the extension of the diagonal of the desired printed size retains the same proportions.

7.23 *Size of the drawing submitted.* It is very desirable for the final drawing submitted to the editor to be exactly the same size as a page of typescript, that is, either 8½ by 11 or 8 by 10½ inches (see sec. 9.12). It can then be handled and shipped with the manuscript, avoiding the use of mailing tubes or other devices to send a large-size figure under separate cover.

Even when the original figure is *small*, it still should be drawn on 8½ by 11 (or 8 by 10½) inch paper. When *large* original drawings are required to secure accuracy, the author should have them photographed and should submit reduced 8½ by 11 (or 8 by 10½) inch glossy prints, mounted if possible on heavy board.

It is helpful to the editor, when such are available to the author, to have glossy prints of figures in the exact reduced size in which they will be printed. Such reduced prints may be submitted in addition to the larger drawings or prints, described above, which are to be sent to the printer. They do not replace the larger drawings.

7.3 Construction of Graphs

7.31 *Drawing paper.* The best material for the original drawing is a blank piece of heavy illustration board. Drawings on cross-section paper are not recommended and are definitely not acceptable if the cross-section lines will photograph and appear in the final figure. Blue-lined grids do not photograph. If the author uses cross-section paper in his original drawing, it is recommended that he submit glossy-print photographs of his figures to the editor.

7.32 *Selection of coordinates.* In general, the independent variable is plotted on the horizontal axis, and the dependent variable on the vertical axis.

7.33 *Laying out the grid.* The next step in plotting the points in a graph is to determine the grid that is to be used. The grid depends on the range and scale separations to be used on the vertical and horizontal axes, and these are in turn determined by the purpose of the graph and the previously determined over-all dimensions. Thus, if the purpose is to show the relationship between two curves obtained under different conditions, it is essential that the vertical units be sufficiently large in separation to show clearly the separation of the curves. Many times it is desirable to begin the vertical units at some value above zero, in order to secure appropriate proportions. When the scale is interrupted, the zero should be indicated on the vertical axis opposite its junction with the horizontal axis, and the vertical axis should be broken with a jagged line a short distance above zero. A similar device to indicate discontinuity should be used on the horizontal axis when that scale does not start at zero, or when there is a break which is not otherwise labeled. In "stretching out" scales, care must be taken not to mislead the reader by magnifying slight differences beyond their real significance.

7.34 *Inking grid lines.* The points of origin of the grid lines along the vertical and horizontal axes should always be inked, with black India ink, precisely opposite the numerical or other scale designation. It is rarely necessary, however, to ink the entire grid of the graph. When it is considered desirable to ink the entire grid, this should be done only for the major divisions of the grid, and should always be done with fine lines which will be just legible in the printed figure. These should be inked only after the entire graph, including printed legends within the graph space, has been inked, in order that the grid lines may be broken around such printed legends and other points in the graph where they might obscure the primary curves. Figure 3 shows a well-drawn graph in which the grid lines have been inked.

7.35 *Plotting points, lines, and curves.* The plotting of experimental points on the graphs should be done with great accuracy. An error in

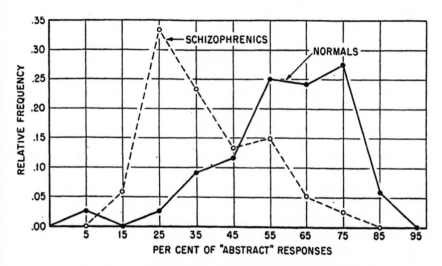

Fig. 3. Example of a well-prepared graph on which some grid lines have lbeen inked Note that the grid lines are broken so that they do not intersect the graph ines or the lettering The original drawing of this graph was twice the reproduced size. The lettering was don·e by a Leroy lettering guide. The data are fictitious; if they were real data presented in an article, an appropriate figure caption might be as follows:

"Fig. 3. Distribution of the abstract responses of the schizophrenic and normal groups."

plotting a point is as significant as an erroneous numerical entry in a table, especially when the graph is used as a substitute for tabular material and may be used by the reader to obtain numerical values. The experimentally obtained points should usually be connected by straight lines, drawn in black India ink. When some demonstrable law, the mathematical statement of which is known, underlies the phenomenon, or where the results have been smoothed by some stated procedure, it is customary to represent the smoothed or generalized curve by a continuous line and to indicate the actual observations by small circles, triangles, or squares. Such smoothed curves should be carefully inked with the aid of drafting instruments.

7.36 *Differentiation of lines.* Each experimental point plotted should be indicated by a small circle made with a drop pen. If two classes of data or curves are plotted on a single graph, they may be best differentiated by leaving open the circles for one class and filling the circles of the other. Further differentiation may be given by connecting one set of circles with a solid line and the other set with a dash line. When more than two classes of data are shown on a single graph, the points may be differentiated by using open and filled squares or triangles to indicate the points, and by using connecting lines of small dots, long and short dashes, dots and dashes, etc. The author should be careful to make the connecting lines clearly distinguishable. Also, the sizes of the circles, etc. used to indicate the plotted points, and the thicknesses of the connecting lines, should be sufficient to allow for the reduction of the graph when the cut is made for printing. Figure 4 shows a graph with differentiated lines.

7.37 *Bar graphs.* Although bar graphs have a definite function in the presentation of data, it should be remembered that they merely translate numerical quantity into visual extent. In the interests of conservation of space, they can rarely be justified in scientific—as contrasted with popular—publications if they present data which appear elsewhere in numerical form, and if the comparisons are sufficiently simple for an expert to grasp immediately in their numerical form. If used, the question whether the bars should extend vertically or horizontally is a matter for the author to decide in view of the scales employed. However, as with other graphs, the independent variable is usually on the horizontal axis and the dependent variable is on the vertical axis. Whenever bar diagrams are used, the frequencies, percentages, or other numerical values that the bars represent should be indicated on the graph.

7.4 Lettering the Graph

7.41 *Planning the lettering.* All numbering or lettering of the grid points on the horizontal *and* vertical axes should be horizontal. The legend for the horizontal scale should, of course, be lettered along a line parallel with that axis. The legend for the vertical axis should be lettered along a vertical line parallel with that axis, because horizontal lettering of the vertical legend would be wasteful of space. Lettering within the graph space is desirable when the graph contains two or more sets of data that require differentiation. It is usually best done by gathering such internal legends in the upper or lower right-hand corner of the graph (Fig. 4). When only two classes of data appear in the graph it is sometimes more effective to insert the legend in close proximity to the referenced curve, with a short arrow pointing to a section of the curve (Fig. 3). The legends should be descriptive of the class of data, e.g., *0-Min. Rest, 10-Min. Rest, Shock Group*, whenever possible, rather than arbitrary designations, e.g., *Group A, Group 61*, etc., which require refer-

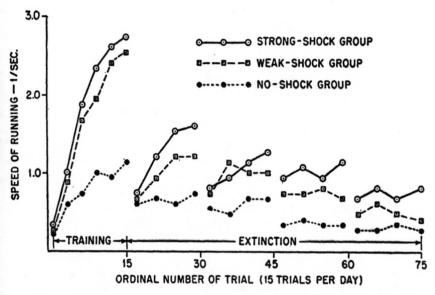

Fig. 4. Example of a graph with differentiated lines. The legend showing the meaning of each type of line is drawn and lettered within the figure area, at the upper right. The data are fictitious. If they were real data presented in an article, the caption might be:

"Fig. 4. The effect of shock on speed of running."

ence to the text. Under no circumstances should the legend be outside the graph space defined by the coordinates. If the legend is too cumbersome to be contained within the graph, the graph should probably be reorganized.

7.42 *Quality of lettering.* The lettering on a graph accepted for publication must be neat, regular, and well spaced. Legends typewritten on an ordinary typewriter are unsatisfactory in appearance and will not be accepted, although special electric typewriters and the Varityper produce a printlike lettering that is excellent. Freehand lettering in black India ink done by a really expert draftsman is good, but amateur freehand lettering almost always lacks regularity of form, line, size, and spacing and cannot be accepted.

The author will insure acceptance of his graphs if he has them lettered in block type with the aid of a lettering guide.

The most widely used lettering guides are the Wrico Lettering Guides, the Leroy System, and the Ames Lettering Device. A set of such guides, suitable for the preparation of graphs for journal publication, should be standard equipment in a psychological laboratory. A novice can, with the aid of these guides, produce professional appearing copy after very little practice. Guides for the same style of block lettering may be obtained in several sizes.

7.43 *Size of lettering.* The size of lettering is a crucial issue. Many graphs have to be printed in wastefully large size because their smallest lettering would be illegible if they were reproduced otherwise.

To determine the size of lettering for a drawn figure, an author may measure the height of a printed capital letter in the usual type size of the journal of his choice. The height of the printed letter is multiplied by the proportion of enlargement of the drawn graph over the printed figure to obtain the correct size of lettering.

If a graph is drawn two linear times its printed size, as suggested in sec. 7.22, words and numerals should be lettered about 5/32 to 3/16 inch high to harmonize with the printed type. Lettering devices have guides for that size.

All lettering on a figure may be of the same size. If two sizes of lettering seem needed, the larger size should not be more than 25 to 50 per cent higher than the smaller size. A printed page does not use type that varies greatly in size, and a figure with some lettering several times as large as some other lettering will be conspicuously inharmonious. In such a case, if the smallest lettering is legible, the largest will be grossly out of proportion.

7.5 *Reproduction of Photographs*

All photographs are reproduced by making a copy on metal, called a *halftone*, of the original furnished by the author. Invariably some detail is lost in making halftones, so that only photographs of good depth of focus and great contrast should be furnished. This detail is best accomplished by a professional photographer, but for those who make their own, one simple consideration deserves more attention than it gets: apparatus should be moved to a neutral background, or a backdrop of blankets or drapes should be hung. A little attention to composition can vastly improve the appearance. Halftones are expensive: if worth while at all, some care should go into their preparation. Line drawings should be substituted wherever possible.

A photograph should be inspected in detail by using four sheets of white paper to form a border which can be shifted until the best composition is selected. Use no more area than is needed, even if it is only a portion of the original print. Indicate the limits of this area on the borders of the print and mark "crop here," but do not cut the photograph yourself. In general, the horizontal dimension as it appears in print should be about two-thirds the width of an entire line of type. Best results are obtained from a "glossy" or ferrotyped print. The maker of the print should know that it is for reproduction by halftone. Any retouching should be done before the ferrotyping. During the last few years, retouching of photographs by the airbrush technique has come into wide use and assists greatly in emphasizing and delineating critical parts of apparatus. The process requires highly skilled technicians, who may be found in most large cities.

7.6 Figure Captions

7.61 *Numbering figures.* All figures, whether graphs, drawings of apparatus, halftones, or what not, are numbered consecutively in arabic numerals throughout an article. For the designation of figures to be deposited with the ADI, see sec. 6.21.

All such cuts are designated as figures. Terms such as "Graph 1" or "Chart 1" are not used. In rare cases when special full-page illustrations are used in a series separate from the other figures, they may be designated as "Plate 1," "Plate 2," etc.

In the text, always refer to figures by their numbers, e.g., "(see Fig. 1)." Never cite "the following" figure, or the figure "above" or "below." It is permissible to abbreviate figure as Fig., except when the word begins a sentence.

7.62 *Showing location of figure.* In the text, show the location of each figure by a clear break in the typewriting, with instructions set off by lines above and below, like this:

Insert Figure 1 about here

7.63 *Typewritten figure captions.* The numbers and captions of figures are *never* lettered on the graph itself. Titles and captions are typewritten in paragraph form, and double spaced if more than one line is required, on a separate sheet or sheets. Titles for several figures should be typed on a single sheet if possible; each caption does *not* have to be on a separate page.

See Fig. 3 and 4 for examples of the appropriate form for figure captions. Note that each caption begins with a paragraph indention, that the word *Figure* is abbreviated *Fig.*, and that the caption is typed in small letters only, without extra capitalization.

Titles should be kept as short as possible, and should not contain explanatory notes which duplicate the legends of the graph or the explanations in the text. It should be remembered that the figure is introduced as an elucidation of the text, and although the graph itself should contain all necessary identifying legends, its interpretation assumes the reading of the text.

7.64 *Identification of the figure.* On the margin of the back of every drawing and photograph submitted, the author should write lightly in pencil his name, the title of the article, and the figure number. These entries identify the figure to the printer. Be careful that the writing does not deface the front of the figure.

If there is any possible ambiguity, as in the case of figures that have no lettering, the author should write *top* lightly in pencil just above the drawing, to show its spatial orientation.

7.65 *Duplicate figures.* To facilitate referral to consulting editors, the figures as well as the typewritten parts of manuscripts must be submitted in duplicate. The original figures must be fully prepared for reproduction according to the instructions given in this section of the *Manual.* The duplicate figures should preferably be photographic or photostatic copies, but clear pencil-drawn drafts are also acceptable as duplicates.

8. *References*

The list of references is placed at the end of an article. Authors should list every reference that is cited in the text of the article, but should not attempt a further compilation of the literature in an area unless the article is primarily a review of literature.

8.1 *Accuracy of Citation*

Accuracy in citations is of major importance. The purpose of listing the references is to make possible their use by the reader; this cannot be accomplished if the reference data are incorrect or incomplete. The working list of references should be checked against the original publications. If original sources are unavailable, yet the reference is important enough to be included, the secondary source from which it was secured should also be indicated. Special attention should be given to spelling of proper names, spelling of words in foreign languages including accents or other special marks, journal abbreviations, years, volume numbers, and pages.

8.2 Arrangement of References

8.21 *Heading.* The correct heading for a list of books and articles cited is *References.* In special cases where the article is a review and some effort is made to exhaust the literature on a subject, or for a designated time period, the heading *Bibliography* may be used.

8.22 *Authors' names.* The basic plan of arrangement of entries is alphabetically by author's surname, or for multiple authors by the name of the senior.

a. Names are given in inverted order—the surname first, followed by the initial or initials. In typing, each initial is followed by a period *and a space.* Failure to space between initials is a common error.

b. For male authors, give the initial or initials only. This rule is followed for male authors with only a single given name (e.g., Paine, T., *not* Paine, Thomas).

c. For female authors, give the full first name, and the middle initial, if used in the publication cited. If a female author has only a single given name, follow it by a period (e.g., Dix, Dorothy.). For married women, use the name as given in the publication cited.

The *Journal of Experimental Psychology* uses only the initials of female authors. The other journals cite the entire first name.

d. In the case of multiple authorship, the inverted order is used for all names, with each name separated from the preceding by a comma. The final name is preceded by a comma and an ampersand (&); do *not* spell out the word *and.*

e. References to an author alone stand first, followed by those of which he is the senior (first named) author. References by one senior author and different second authors are arranged alphabetically by the surname of the second author, etc.

f. Several references to the same author or authors are arranged by year of publication, the earlier first. References of the same year are arranged alphabetically by title.

g. The author's name is repeated in each entry. Do *not* replace the name by a dash.

8.23 *Rules for alphabetization.* The following rules govern special cases of alphabetization:

   a. Prefixes M', Mc, and Mac should be alphabetized as though spelled Mac. St. and Ste. should be alphabetized as though spelled out, i.e., Saint.

   b. Compound names are alphabetized under the first part of the name: Kloos-Knies, P., Lewis-Jones, H.

   c. Article and preposition prefixes (de, la, du, von, van der, della, etc.) govern alphabetical position in accordance with different rules for different languages. Inasmuch as the prefix when included in Anglicized usage is commonly spoken as part of the surname, the APA journals alphabetize according to the prefix. In certain names, e.g., [von] Helmholtz, the prefix is not customarily used in English and the alphabetization then disregards it.

   d. Certain languages have roman letters not in the English alphabet—Danish æ, ø, and aa; Norwegian æ, ø, or ö, and å or aa; Swedish å, ä, and ö; and Spanish ch, ll, rr, and ñ. Strict rules would require proper alphabetization of these letters according to their language, but practical considerations have dictated that the APA journals alphabetize them as though they were accented variations of roman letters. This practice is analogous to usage for transliterations from nonroman alphabets.

8.24 *Entries with no personal author.* Entries to publications for which no person is indicated as author may be divided into three classes: (*a*) corporate author indicated, (*b*) article signed *Anonymous*, and (*c*) neither of the preceding.

a. When a *corporate author* is clearly indicated, the accepted practice follows. Rules for such entries were published by Louttit (**17**), and examples will be found in the list of references at the end of this manual, items numbered 1, 2, 3, 16, 21, 22, and 23.

   i. A corporate author may be an association or subdivision of one, a governmental agency, a business firm, etc.

   ii. The full official title of the corporate body should be used, e.g., American Psychological Association, Psychological Corporation, U. S. Department of Defense.

   iii. A subdivision of a larger unit is entered with the larger body first and the subdivision following, e.g., American Psychological Association, Policy and Planning Board. In the case of government agencies, the name or abbreviation of the nation, state, or city appears first.

   iv. Corporate authors are arranged in proper alphabetical position with personal authors.

b. Articles specifically signed *Anonymous* are arranged with this word as name entry in the alphabetical list.

c. Entries for which no author is evident should be arranged by title (disregarding the articles *the, a, an*) in the alphabetical list. Examples will be found in the list of references of this manual, items numbered 5, 25, and 28.

8.25 *Numbering references.* The references are numbered consecutively with arabic numbers, each number being followed by a period and not placed in parentheses. See the *References* at the end of this manual. If a reference is added at a late stage in the preparation of the average manuscript, authors should renumber all of the references which follow, and correct the citation numbers in the text. In very long bibliographies, where an addition at the beginning of the list would require a major number of changes in the list and the text, an interpolated number (e.g., "13*a*") may be used.

8.3 *Forms of Book Entries*

The entry should contain all data necessary for identification and library search.

Most of the needed instructions can be obtained from the examples which follow. A few special directions are:

a. Place of publication. Give only the city if the name is distinctive and well known. Give the city and state if there are several cities of that name (e.g., Springfield, Ill.), or if the city is obscure. If the publisher is a rarely known one, his street address may be given in parentheses, following the city and state.

b. Publisher's name. Give in as brief a form as will be fully intelligible, e.g., *McGraw-Hill,* not *McGraw-Hill Book Co.*

c. Citing pages. Particular pages of a book, except for the entire pages of a chapter having separate authorship, are never cited in the reference list. Specific page references required to identify a quotation are given in parentheses in the text (see sec. 4.71 and 4.76).

In the following illustrations, all authors' names and titles are fictitious.

8.31 *Book.*

Jefferds, C. V., Jr. *The psychology of industrial unrest.* New York: McGraw-Hill, 1951.

8.32 *New edition.* Note that *edition* is abbreviated (ed.).

Jefferds, C. V., Jr. *The psychology of industrial unrest.* (2nd ed.) New York: McGraw-Hill, 1955.

8.33 *Edited book.* Note that *editor* is abbreviated (Ed.).

Rodner, A. H. (Ed.) *Theories of psychopathology.* Springfield, Ill.: Charles C Thomas, 1945.

8.34 *Specific chapter in edited book.*

Stansill, Dora. The reinforcement of anxiety. In A. H. Rodner (Ed.), *Theories of psychopathology.* Springfield, Ill.: Charles C Thomas, 1945. Pp. 50–93.

8.35 *Work of several volumes.*

Lochren, H. R. *Collected works.* London: Oxford Univer. Press, 1938–40. 4 vols.

8.36 *Reference to one volume of multivolume work.*

Patwell, E. D., Whiston, Anita J., & Gresser, T. M. *Guide to intelligence examinations.* Vol. 1. *Principles.* Boston: Houghton Mifflin, 1947.

8.37 *Author as publisher.* (May be used for personal or corporate author.)

Branam, F. P. *A new theory of taste.* Chicago: Author, 1954.

Consulting Psychologists, Inc. *Program of supervisory training.* Boston: Author, 1951.

8.38 *Book with author's name in title.*

Neckerman, S. F. *Collected papers of.* . . . New York: Roidan Press, 1948.

8.4 *Form of Periodical Entries*

8.41 *Journal article, pagination by volume.*

Archer, P. W. The tactile perception of roughness. *Amer. J. Psychol.*, 1950, **63**, 365–373.

8.42 *Journal article, pagination by issue.* The issue number is cited in parentheses, following the volume number, only when each issue has independent pagination.

Cardinal, M. H. Anxiety among displaced children. *Bull. World Fed. ment. Hlth*, 1950, **2** (4), 27–35.

8.43 *Monograph, with volume number, issue number, and serial (whole) number.*

Follette, Jane. The relation of intelligence to motor skill. *Psychol. Monogr.*, 1950, **62**, No. 14 (Whole No. 287).

8.44 *Monograph, without volume number.*

Merwede, D. R. Measurement of teachers' attitudes. *Teach. Coll. Contr. Educ.*, 1950, No. 643.

8.45 *Yearbook.* (For chapter in a Yearbook, see also 8.34.)

Schwam, C. W. (Ed.) Mental health in education. *Yearb. nat. Soc. Stud. Educ.*, 1952, 51, Part II.

8.46 *Citation of an abstract.*

Newell, N. B. Vocabulary as a function of adult age. *Amer. Psychologist*, 1951, **6**, 420. (Abstract)

8.47 *Citation from secondary source.* While references should whenever possible be checked with the original, in a few instances pertinent material is available only from a secondary source. Inclusion of such references is permissible with the secondary source indicated.

Harkavy-Katz, S. Hayelod hahole b'shituk mohi v'hayeled hamongoloidi b'hayey hamishpaha. *Harefuah*, 1952, **43**, 70–71. (*Psychol. Abstr.*, 28:1182)

Smithers, E. F. Mating behavior of *Bufo. Midland Pap. nat. Hist.*, 1872, **6**, 4–8. Cited by A. N. Gora, *Amphibian biology*. London: Baker & Smith, 1949. P. 63.

8.5 *Government reports.*

The bibliography of reports from governmental agencies, especially the near-print reports of research projects, is exceedingly complex. No simple rules for citation can be formulated. *Psychological Abstracts* has used bibliographic entries of the book or journal article form with the addition of identifying data such as Project Number, Contract Number, or the name of the contractor. The basic principle is to give sufficient information so that the interested reader may secure a copy from a library or the issuing agency. A practical suggestion to authors is to cite such reports as they have been cited in *Psychological Abstracts*.

8.6 *Citation of Unpublished Materials*

8.61 *Dissertations.*

Lightburn, L. T. The relation of critical fusion frequency to age. Unpublished doctoral dissertation, Univer. of New Jersey, 1951.

8.62 *Other unpublished manuscripts.* These should not be cited unless the manuscript is on file with the ADI or available from a library. Give author, title, the words *Unpublished manuscript* (which are not underlined), the library from which available or the ADI document number, and the date.

8.63 *Paper read at a meeting.* Citation should be to an abstract if one has been published. If there is no published abstract and it is essential to cite the paper, cite it as follows:

Overpeck, R. A. Partial reinforcement in relation to extinction. Paper read at Midwest. Psychol. Ass., Chicago, April, 1949.

8.64 *Personal communication.* A letter or informally transmitted document is better acknowledged in a footnote than in a reference list.

If cited, give the name, the words *Personal communication* (which are not underlined), and end with a period, and the date.

8.65 *Article "in press."* An article accepted for publication but not yet in print may be designated as "in press." To cite such an article give author, exact title of article, the abbreviation for the name of the journal, and then the words *in press* which are not underlined or placed in quotation marks. Such a reference can often be completed by the time that the author receives proof.

Sedlack, J. A. Rorschach indicators of anxiety. *J. consult. Psychol.*, in press.

8.66 *Article "in preparation."* Contemplated or unfinished articles do not belong in a reference list, as they are not yet a part of the professional literature. Therefore, articles "in preparation" should not be cited.

8.7 Journal Citations

The APA publications use the abbreviations of journal titles that appear in the *World List of Scientific Periodicals* (28). These abbreviations are based on a code adopted by the International Institute of Intellectual Cooperation of the League of Nations (16). The essence of the code is reproduced below, and actual usage can be found in the "List of Journals Abstracted" published in the index number of *Psychological Abstracts* since Volume 21, 1947.

8.71 *Rules for abbreviation.* For convenience, the following rules adapted from the official code are presented:

a. Abbreviations should not be beyond a point of easy identification.

b. Abridged form includes all words except articles, conjunctions, prepositions, etc. Exceptions: (i) retain the connective in a title of only two nouns, e.g., *Sci. & Soc.;* (ii) retain the conjunction between two compound nouns the last part of which is common to both, e.g., Land-und fortswirtschaftliche Blatter, *Land-u. fortsw. Bl.;* (iii) omit additional less important words in exceptionally long titles, e.g., Comptes rendus hebdomadaires des séances de l'Academie des Sciences, *C. R. Acad. Sci., Paris.*

c. Abbreviations may be made by omitting terminal letters or by contraction. If the terminal letter is omitted, the abbreviation ends in a period, e.g., Psychology, *Psychol.*, Development, *Develpm.*, etc. If the terminal letter remains, there is no period, e.g., Health, *Hlth*, Measurement, *Measmt*, etc.

d. Abbreviation is the same for singular and plural forms.

e. Nouns are capitalized and adjectives are not. Thus adjectives from nominatives have the same abbreviation but with the initial letter in small letters, e.g., Psychology, *Psychol.;* psychological, *psychol.*

f. Cognate words in different languages are reduced to the same form when orthography permits, e.g., *Acad., Accad., Akad.*

g. Single word titles are not abbreviated.

h. Parts of compound words are abbreviated as when standing alone: the parts are connected by a hyphen or in German words by a second capital, e.g., medicolegal, *med.-leg.;* Arbeitswissenschaft, *ArbWiss.*

i. If the title of a journal includes a personal name, only the surname is used. Proper surnames in journal titles are not abbreviated.

j. Place is indicated only (i) to distinguish two journals of same name; (ii) when the abbreviation does not reveal the language used; (iii) if the title is in a language other than that of the country of publication.

k. Science names ending in "ology" or its foreign language variants omit the "ogy," e.g., Neurology, *Neurol.* Those ending in "ics" omit the ending, e.g., Optics. *Opt.*

8.72 *Examples.* The following list includes major American psychological journals, including some no longer published, and other titles which illustrate special rules. A more complete list of titles and abbreviations will be found in the annual index of *Psychological Abstracts.*

Advanced Management	*Advanc. Mgmt*
American Journal of Mental Deficiency	*Amer. J. ment. Defic.*
American Journal of Orthopsychiatry	*Amer. J. Orthopsychiat.*
American Journal of Psychology	*Amer. J. Psychol.*
American Psychologist	*Amer. Psychologist*
Année Psychologique	*Année psychol.*
Annual Review of Psychology	*Annu. Rev. Psychol.*
Archives de Psychologie, Genève	*Arch. Psychol., Genève*
Archives of Psychology, New York	*Arch. Psychol., N. Y.*
Canadian Journal of Psychology	*Canad. J. Psychol.*
Character and Personality	*Charact. & Pers.*
Child Development	*Child Develpm.*
Contemporary Psychology	*Contemp. Psychol.*
Educational and Psychological Measurement	*Educ. psychol. Measmt*
Genetic Psychology Monographs	*Genet. Psychol. Monogr.*
Journal of Abnormal and Social Psychology	*J. abnorm. soc. Psychol.*
Journal of the Acoustical Society of America	*J. acoust. Soc. Amer.*
Journal of Applied Psychology	*J. appl. Psychol.*
Journal of Clinical Psychology	*J. clin. Psychol.*
Journal of Comparative and Physiological Psychology	*J. comp. physiol. Psychol.*
Journal of Consulting Psychology	*J. consult. Psychol.*
Journal of Counseling Psychology	*J. counsel. Psychol.*
Journal of Educational Psychology	*J. educ. Psychol.*
Journal of Experimental Psychology	*J. exp. Psychol.*
Journal of General Psychology	*J. gen. Psychol.*
Journal of Genetic Psychology	*J. genet. Psychol.*
Journal of the Optical Society of America	*J. opt. Soc. Amer.*
Journal of Personality	*J. Pers.*
Journal of Projective Techniques	*J. proj. Tech.*
Journal de Psychologie Normale et Pathologique	*J. Psychol. norm. path.*
Journal of Psychology	*J. Psychol.*
Journal of Social Issues	*J. soc. Issues*

Journal of Social Psychology	*J. soc. Psychol.*
Mental Hygiene	*Ment. Hyg., N. Y.*
Perceptual and Motor Skills	*Percept. mot. Skills*
Personnel Psychology	*Personnel Psychol.*
Pflügers Archiv für die gesamte Physiologie	
des Menschen und die Tiere	*Pflüg. Arch. ges. Physiol.*
Psychological Abstracts	*Psychol. Abstr.*
Psychological Bulletin	*Psychol. Bull.*
Psychological Monographs: General and Applied	*Psychol. Monogr.*
Psychological Review	*Psychol. Rev.*
Psychometrika	*Psychometrika*
Revue de Psychologie	*Rev. Psychol., Montreal*
Rorschach Research Exchange	*Rorschach Res. Exch.*

8.73 *A list of abbreviations.* The citations of most of the widely used journals can be obtained by appropriate combination of the following abbreviations:

Abhandlungen	*Abh.*	Casework	*Casewk*
abnormal	*abnorm.*	Character	*Charact.*
Abstract	*Abstr.*	Childhood	*Childh.*
Academy, Academie,		Children	*Child.*
Academia	*Acad.*	Clinic	*Clin.*
Accademia	*Accad.*	clinical	*clin.*
Akademie	*Akad.*	College	*Coll.*
allgemeine, allgemeiner	*allg.*	comparative	*comp.*
American	*Amer.*	Comptes-rendus	*C.R.*
Anales	*An.*	Conference	*Conf.*
angewandte	*angew.*	Congress	*Congr.*
Annals, Annaes, Annale,		consulting	*consult.*
Annalen, Annali	*Ann.*	Contribution	*Contr.*
Annual, Annuaire,		counseling	*counsel.*
Annuario	*Annu.*	criminal, criminelle	*crim.*
Anthropology,		Deficiency	*Def.*
Anthropologie	*Anthrop.*	Delinquent, Delinquency	*Delinqu.*
Anzeiger	*Anz.*	Department	*Dep.*
applied, appliquées	*appl.*	Deutsche	*Dtsch.*
Arbeitswissenschaft	*ArbWiss.*	Development	*Develpm.*
Archives, Archivio,		Digest	*Dig.*
Archivos, Archiv,		Disease	*Dis.*
Archivo	*Arch.*	eastern	*east.*
Asociación	*Asoc.*	Education	*Educ.*
Association	*Ass.*	Employment	*Emplyt*
Behavior	*Behav.*	Engineer	*Engr*
Beihefte	*Beih.*	Engineering	*Engng*
Bericht	*Ber.*	Ergebnisse	*Ergebn.*
Board	*Bd*	Evolution	*Evolut.*
Bulletin	*Bull.*	exceptional	*except.*

Exchange	*Exch.*	normal	*norm.*
experimental,		North	*N.*
experimentelle,		northern	*north.*
experimentale	*exp.*	occupational	*occup.*
Family	*Fam.*	Opinion	*Opin.*
Forschung	*Forsch.*	Orthopsychiatry	*Orthopsychiat.*
Fortschritte	*Fortschr.*	Pathology	*Path.*
Foundation	*Found.*	Pedagogy	*Pedag.*
Gegenwart	*Gegenw.*	Personality	*Pers.*
general, generale, géneral	*gen.*	Personnel	*Personnel*
genetic	*genet.*	Philosophy	*Phil.*
Gerontology	*Geront.*	Phonetics	*Phon.*
gesamte	*ges.*	Practice	*Pract.*
Gesellschaft	*Ges.*	Practitioner	*Practit.*
Handbook, Handbuch	*Handb.*	Press	*Pr.*
Health	*Hlth*	Proceedings	*Proc.*
Heredity	*Hered.*	Progress	*Progr.*
Illumination	*Illum.*	projective	*proj.*
Individual	*Indiv.*	Psychiatry	*Psychiat.*
industrial	*industr.*	psychical	*psych.*
Institute, Institut,		Psychoanalysis	*Psychoanal.*
Instituto	*Inst.*	Psychology	*Psychol.*
Institution	*Instn*	Psychometrics	*Psychometr.*
Instrument	*Instrum.*	Psychopathology	*Psychopath.*
internal	*intern.*	psychosomatic	*psychosom.*
international	*int.*	Psychotechnics	*Psychotech.*
Investigation	*Invest.*	Psychotherapy	*Psychother.*
Jahrbuch	*Jb.*	Public	*Publ.*
Journal	*J.*	Publication	*Publ.*
Journalism	*Journ.*	quantitative	*quant.*
juvenile	*juv.*	quarterly	*quart.*
Kwartalnik	*Kwart.*	Record	*Rec.*
Laboratory	*Lab.*	Rehabilitation	*Rehabilit.*
Measurement	*Measmt*	Relations	*Relat.*
mechanical	*mech.*	Religion	*Relig.*
Management	*Mgmt*	Report	*Rep.*
Medicine	*Med.*	Research	*Res.*
medicolegal	*med.-leg.*	Review, Revista, Revue	*Rev.*
Memoir	*Mem.*	Rivista	*Riv.*
mental	*ment.*	School	*Sch.*
Miscellaneous	*Misc.*	Schriften	*Schr.*
Monatsschrift	*Mschr.*	Science	*Sci.*
Monograph	*Monogr.*	Series	*Ser.*
monthly	*mon.*	Service	*Serv.*
Nervenheilkunde	*Nervenheilk.*	social	*soc.*
nervous	*nerv.*	Society	*Soc.*
Neuropathology	*Neuropath.*	South	*S.*
Newsletter	*Newsltr*	southern	*sth.*

special	*spec.*	University	*Univer.*
sperimentale	*sper.*	Untersuchungen	*Untersuch.*
Statistics	*Statist.*	vergleichende	*vergl.*
Study, Studies, Studien	*Stud.*	vocational	*voc.*
Supervision	*Supervis.*	Weekly	*Wkly*
Supplement	*Suppl.*	Welfare	*Welf.*
Survey	*Surv.*	western	*west.*
Symposium	*Sympos.*	Wissenschaft	*Wiss.*
technical	*tech.*	Wochenschrift	*Wschr.*
Theory	*Theor.*	Work	*Wk*
Therapy	*Ther.*	Yearbook	*Yearb.*
Training	*Train.*	Zeitschrift	*Z.*
Transactions	*Trans.*	Zentralblatt	*Zbl.*
und	*u.*	Zhurnal	*Zh.*

8.8 Typing the References

8.81 *Double space.* References should be double spaced between each and every line, not just between the references. The extra spacing is needed for editor's marks.

8.82 *Capitalization.* Only the initial letter of the first word of the title of a book or article is capitalized. Of course, regular capitalization rules also hold: proper names, German nouns, etc.

Authors' names are typed in large and small letters, not in all capitals.

8.83 *Punctuation.* Special attention must be paid to uniformity and accuracy of punctuation.

Titles are *not* enclosed in quotation marks.

8.84 *Italics.* Book titles, and the abbreviations of journals, should be single underlined to indicate italics. Do not underline any other matter.

9. Typing the Manuscript

The typing of a manuscript is a most important step. The author should study this section carefully and go over it in detail with his typist. Many shortcomings of manuscripts result from failure to observe a few simple rules for typing. Papers often have to be returned to authors because of lack of double spacing or lack of sufficiently wide margins.

9.1 General Requirements of Typing

9.11 *Submit manuscript in duplicate.* Manuscripts must be submitted in duplicate, to facilitate referral to consulting editors. One copy must be an original typewritten copy, typed on one side of the paper only. The duplicate should be the first, clear, carbon copy.

The final copy must be neat. The typewriter ribbon should make a dark, even impression, and the machine should be in good mechanical condition to provide accurate spacing, alignment, and clean-cut letters. Clean the typewriter keys so that clear differences can be seen between letters such as *c*, *e*, and *o*, and between numerals such as *3* and *8*.

Psychological Monographs will accept clear carbon copies of pages from doctoral dissertations.

Mimeographed or hectographed copy is usually not desirable, but in special circumstances it will be considered. Such copy should be clear and legible, and typed with double spacing. Figures and other material for photographic reproduction in such copy cannot be used.

9.12 *Use heavy paper of standard size.* Manuscripts should be typed on heavy bond paper of good quality. Tissue, onion skin, and thin "airmail" paper should not be used, because they will not stand the stresses of handling, and because their transparency reduces legibility.

Only paper of 8½ by 11 inches (standard) or 8 by 10½ inches (government) size should be used. All sheets of one manuscript must be of the same size.

Use no part-sheets, "flyers," or strips of paper glued, pinned, or stapled to the sheet. They are often torn off or lost in shipment and handling.

9.13 *Leave wide margins.* Leave a margin of one inch or more at the top, bottom, right, and left of every page. The editor has to write many instructions to the printer in the margins.

It is helpful to type every line as nearly six inches long as possible. Set a pica typewriter to a 60-character line, an elite machine to 72 characters. Uniformity helps the editor to make a more exact estimate of the length of the article.

9.14 *Indent all paragraphs.* Indent the first line of every paragraph, including footnotes. Do not use a "block" form for typing.

Type *all* of a manuscript to the same uniform left-hand margin, except for the paragraph indentions. Do not give extra indention to quotations or other matter to be set in smaller type. Do not indent whole paragraphs to give them emphasis. Do not use, in the text of an article, an outline form that has graduated indentions. The journals print all matter to a uniform left margin; any other practice is wasteful of space. It is expensive and monotonous editorial labor to indicate to the printer that extra-indented lines are to be brought to the margin.

9.15 *Double space throughout.* Double space between *all* lines of the manuscript without exception. This is essential in order to maximize legibility and to provide space for editorial corrections. Double spacing means making a double space between every line in the title, headings, footnotes, quotations, references, and figure captions, and in the tables if possible (see sec. 5.23). A good rule for the typist is: Set the typewriter for double spacing and leave it there!

9.16 *Type no word in all capitals.* Another good typing rule is *never* to type any whole word in all capital letters. Do not type the title of article, the authors' names, centered headings, or table headings in all capitals. Instead, use capital and small letters, capitalizing only the initial letters of important words. Some journals use capital letters for titles and headings, but others do not. It is easier for an editor to add instructions to set matter in capitals than for him to indicate the removal of undesired capitals.

9.17 *Underline sparingly.* Use an underline only when you mean to set a word in italics, and use italics very infrequently (see sec. 4.3).

9.18 *Use separate sheets for tables, captions, and references.* Type each table on a separate sheet of paper. Type figure captions in order, starting on a new sheet (see sec. 7.63). Begin the *References* at the top of a new page.

9.19 *Minimize corrections.* A moderate number of neat typewritten or pen-lettered corrections is acceptable in manuscripts. Manuscripts are corrected between the lines, not in the margins. Never add a sentence written vertically on the manuscript's margins. Strikeovers on the typewriter are not acceptable corrections, as they are often ambiguous. Erase neatly, or make clear correction by pen. If there are many corrections, the manuscript should be retyped.

9.2 *Arrangement of Pages*

Arrange the pages of the manuscript of a journal article as follows:

a. First page, with title, author's name, etc. The text follows immediately on the same page.

b. Pages of text.

c. References (start on a new page).

d. Footnotes (start on a new page).

e. Tables (each on a separate sheet).

f. Figure captions (start on a new page).

g. Figures (each separately).

9.3 *Numbering of Pages*

Number all the pages of a manuscript in a consistent position, preferably in the upper right corner. All manuscript pages, when arranged in the order given in sec. 9.2, must be consecutively numbered with arabic numerals. Note that pages of references, footnotes, tables, and figure captions are numbered, not only the text pages.

In short manuscripts such as those prepared for journal articles there should be no need to insert pages numbered "*6a*" and the like. If an additional page is inserted after the pages have once been numbered, renumber all the pages.

Since pages might become separated at the printers, it is also wise to identify each manuscript page by typing the senior author's last name in its upper left-hand corner.

9.4 *Wrapping and Shipping*

The protection of the manuscript from the rough handling it may receive in transit is often neglected by authors. The mailing envelope should be strong and provided with a stiff cardboard or corrugated filler slightly smaller than the envelope. The filler is essential if drawings, photographs, or materials intended for ADI are enclosed. A heavy manuscript needs the additional protection of a string tied securely lengthwise and crosswise around the envelope. Authors might be amazed to see the number of manuscripts that reach their destination in torn envelopes and a crumpled condition.

Do not enclose the manuscript in a loose-leaf binder, or staple or fasten the pages together in any way. Binders add unduly to shipping weight, and editors and printers prefer to work with loose sheets.

The author should always retain a second carbon copy of a paper, as a precaution against the loss of the original.

Mail the manuscript to the editor, not to the APA Central Office, except in the case of manuscripts for the *American Psychologist* or for *Psychological Abstracts*, whose offices are located there. It is important to check the current issue of the journal for which the manuscript is being prepared, in order to ascertain the name of the editor and his mailing address; journals change editors from time to time, and editors change addresses.

Council of Editors

10. *Correction of Proofs*

10.1 *Proofreading*

An author's last responsibility is to read the proofs accurately. A month or so before the issue is to appear, each author receives two sets of proofs and the manuscript from the printer. Experienced proofreaders advise the following method:

First, give the proof a "literal" reading. A "copyholder"—your secretary, your wife, a colleague, a student—reads the manuscript aloud slowly in a monotonous voice, reading all punctuation marks, and spelling out all proper names and technical words. Simultaneously, you read the proof, letter by letter and not for sense, to catch all deviations from the manuscript. Read every caption and heading, and every numeral in each table. Mark all corrections on the proof with standard proofreader's marks, which may be found in many standard reference books (6, 20, 23, 25). Most corrections should be indicated in the margins of the proofsheets. Do not try to squeeze corrections between the printed lines. If you have no one to serve as copyholder, you can read proof alone by glancing from the proof to the copy, but it is not nearly as efficient.

Second, read the proofs again carefully for the sense, in the way that you would read an article or book. This reading will reveal broader errors such as the omission of a key sentence which, strange as it seems, you can miss in the literal proofreading.

Third, check specific points: (*a*) Are the title, authors' names, and institutional connections correct? (*b*) Are the tables all printed, and are they reasonably well placed? (c) Are the figures correct? Is the correct caption under each figure? Switched captions under similar figures are not rare. (*d*) Are the centered and paragraph headings correct and correctly placed? (*e*) Finally, look at every hyphenated word at the right-hand edge of each column or page. Are the words divided into syllables correctly? Use a dictionary to check the syllabication of a word when you are not sure.

The author bears the primary responsibility for proofreading, and must not take the task lightly. Promptness is essential. If you do not read and return the proof within a day or two, the printer's schedule is thrown out of gear; he has obligations to other publications as well as to the journal in which your article will appear. A week's delay in returning your proof may mean a longer delay in the appearance of the whole issue. You return one copy of the corrected proof, and the manuscript (that is essential!) to the Managing Editor of APA publications in Washington, according to instructions received with the proof. You keep the other copy of the proof for your own files.

10.2 *Author's Alterations*

Proofreading makes the printed page identical with the manuscript copy, and nothing more. To make a change on the proof other than to make it correspond exactly to the manuscript is an *author's alteration*, which must be avoided except in extreme instances. To strike out or change a single word near the beginning of a paragraph often requires resetting the entire paragraph. The cost is charged to the author. Even worse, extensive author's alterations may cause delays in publication, and may lead to the introduction of errors when the author's intentions are not entirely clear to the printer.

When a change on the proofs is essential—to correct a serious and hitherto undiscovered error of fact or interpretation—it is important to plan the alteration to minimize cost and confusion. To change words at the end of a paragraph, or to add several more lines to the end of a paragraph, costs comparatively little. If a change near the beginning of a paragraph is necessary, the author should count the number of characters and spaces to be removed and make an insertion or change that will use as nearly as possible the same number of characters and spaces. Corrections may not be made in the proofs of figures, as changes cannot be made in the electrotypes. If a change is absolutely necessary, the figure must be completely redrawn and the new copy submitted. The best practice is to have the manuscript so free from errors that alterations on the proof are unnecessary.

Conclusion

The journals of the American Psychological Association are a joint enterprise of their readers, authors, and editors. The value of the journals for the advancement of psychology as a science and profession depends on the quality of the articles prepared by the authors and selected by the editors. This publication manual is a tool for improving techniques of communication.

The editors offer the manual with the hope that every author will consult it before submitting a manuscript for publication, and that departments giving graduate instruction in psychology will require their students to use it as a guide for the preparation of papers.

References

1. American Psychological Association, Council of Editors. Publication manual of the American Psychological Association. *Psychol. Bull.*, 1952, 49, 389–449.
2. American Standards Association, Committee on Standards for Graphic Representation. *Time-series charts: a manual of design and construction, American standard,* *1938.* New York: American Society of Mechanical Engineers, 1938.
3. American Standards Association, Committee on Standards for Graphic Representation. *Engineering and scientific graphs for publication, American standard, 1943.* New York: American Society of Mechanical Engineers, 1943.
4. Arkin, H., & Cotton, R. *Graphs: How*

to make and use them. (2nd ed.) New York: Harper, 1938.

5. *Author's guide.* New York: Wiley, 1950.

6. Barnhart, C. L. (Ed.) *The American college dictionary.* New York: Random House, 1953.

7. Brinton, W. C. *Graphic presentation.* New York: Brinton Associates, 1939.

8. Conrad, H. S. Preparation of manuscripts for publication as monographs. *J. Psychol.*, 1948, **26**, 447–459.

9. Daniel, R. S., & Louttit, C. M. *Professional problems in psychology.* New York: Prentice-Hall, 1953.

10. Dunlap, J. W., & Kurtz, A. K. *Handbook of statistical nomographs, tables, and formulas.* Yonkers, N. Y.: World Book Co., 1932.

11. Flesch, R. *The art of readable writing.* New York: Harper, 1949.

12. Fowler, H. W. *A dictionary of modern English usage.* London: Humphrey Milford, 1936.

13. Haskell, A. C. *How to make and use graphic charts.* New York: Codex Book Co., 1919.

14. Jenkinson, B. L. *Manual of tabular presentation.* Washington: U. S. Government Printing Office, 1939.

15. Kurtz, A. K., & Edgerton, H. A. *Statistical dictionary of terms and symbols.* New York: Wiley, 1939.

16. League of Nations, International Institute of Intellectual Cooperation. *International code of abbreviations for titles of periodicals.* Paris: Author, 1930.

17. Louttit, C. M. *Psychological Abstracts'* policy on corporate author entries.

Amer. Psychologist, 1950, **5**, 673–677.

18. Mawson, C. O. S. (Ed.) *Roget's international thesaurus.* (Rev. ed.) New York: Cromwell, 1946.

19. Parker, W. R. (Ed.) The MLA style sheet. *Publ. mod. Lang. Ass. Amer.*, 1951, **66** (3), 1–31.

20. Skillin, Marjorie E., & Gay, R. M. *Words into type.* New York: Appleton-Century-Crofts, 1948.

21. U. S. Federal Security Agency. *Statistical manual of the Social Security Board.* Washington: U. S. Government Printing Office, 1941.

22. U. S. Government Printing Office. *Style manual.* (1945 rev.) Washington: Author, 1945.

23. University of Chicago Press. *A manual of style.* (11th ed.) Chicago: Author, 1949.

24. Walker, Helen M., & Durost, W. N. *Statistical tables: their structure and use.* New York: Teachers Coll., Columbia Univer., Bureau of Publications, 1936.

25. *Webster's new international dictionary of the English language.* (2nd ed., Unabridged) Springfield, Mass.: G. & C. Merriam, 1934.

26. Williams, J. H. *Graphic methods in education.* Boston: Houghton Mifflin, 1924.

27. Woolley, E. C., & Scott, F. W. *College handbook of composition.* (4th ed.) Boston: Heath, 1944.

28. *A world list of scientific periodicals published in the years 1900–1933.* (2nd ed.) London: Oxford Univer. Press, 1934.

Index

CPSIA information can be obtained at www.ICGtesting.com
Printed in the USA
LVOW06s0026181115

463097LV00001B/28/P